T0194421

A More Elite Man

Major Phil Kramer

WESTBOW
PRESS®
A DIVISION OF THOMAS NELSON
& ZONDERVAN

This book is a work of non-fiction. Unless otherwise noted, the author and the publisher make no explicit guarantees as to the accuracy of the information contained in this book and in some cases, names of people and places have been altered to protect their privacy.

WestBow Press books may be ordered through booksellers or by contacting:

WestBow Press
A Division of Thomas Nelson & Zondervan
1663 Liberty Drive
Bloomington, IN 47403
www.westbowpress.com
1 (866) 928-1240

Because of the dynamic nature of the Internet, any web addresses or links contained in this book may have changed since publication and may no longer be valid. The views expressed in this work are solely those of the author and do not necessarily reflect the views of the publisher or the United States Army, and the publisher and the United States Army hereby disclaim any responsibility for them.

Any people depicted in stock imagery provided by Thinkstock are models, and such images are being used for illustrative purposes only. Certain stock imagery © Thinkstock.

Scripture quotations are from the ESV® Bible (The Holy Bible, English Standard Version®), copyright © 2001 by Crossway, a publishing ministry of Good News Publishers. Used by permission. All rights reserved.

ISBN: 978-1-9736-0940-7 (sc)
ISBN: 978-1-9736-0941-4 (hc)
ISBN: 978-1-9736-0939-1 (e)

Library of Congress Control Number: 2017918417

Print information available on the last page.

WestBow Press rev. date: 11/30/2017

"Be watchful, stand firm in the faith, act like men, be strong!"
(1 Corinthians 16:13)

Contents

Introduction ix

1   Life Navigation: Finding Your Way to God's High Ground 1

2   Discipline: Self-Leadership Precedes Team-Leadership 23

3   Team Leadership: A Man's Highest Calling 45

4   I Will Always Endeavor: Fear God and Take Your Own Part 60

5   My Care of Equipment: Financial Wisdom in a Foolish World . 94

6   Spiritual Athlete Warrior: Personal Training in God's Gym 114

7   Your Dad's Leadership: The Good, the Bad, and the Ugly 149

8   Give Way Together: The Commander's Intent for Your Marriage 164

9   Fathers Lead the Way: Developing Influence With Your Kids .. 182

10   How to Get a GO with God: The Greatest Question a Man Will Ever Answer 200

Introduction

"I wanna be an Airborne Ranger!"

Visit any Army post across the globe during morning physical training and you're bound to hear soldiers singing those words while running down the street. Regardless of duty position, rank, or even gender, soldiers everywhere acknowledge that Rangers occupy the pinnacle of the Army's warfighting pyramid.

Army Rangers are amazing soldiers. They are mentally alert and physically strong. On land, sea, or air, they move further, faster, and fight harder than any other soldier. They are specially selected, well trained, and give one-hundred percent and then some to every task. And, because of the challenges they overcome every day, Rangers possess an unusually high esprit-de-corps in their ranks.

As you might imagine, the Rangers attract a certain kind of man. While many new Army recruits look primarily for a paycheck or some kind of vocational training perhaps with little motivation to go above and beyond the minimum requirements, Rangers overwhelmingly prove to be highly-motivated self-starters who naturally seek personal challenges. Consider, for example, the numerous physical, mental, and tactical hurdles that stand between a young soldier and the coveted title of "Army Ranger." Even among the highly motivated, many will fall by the wayside before completing the mission. And let's not forget that after they reach that milestone, Rangers face a lifetime of living up to the title every day of their lives.

Who are these soldiers who give one-hundred percent and then some to become Rangers? By and large, they are type-A men who want to get the most out of life. They are not satisfied merely with surviving; they want to thrive—to squeeze every drop out of their days on this earth. Driven by a desire to excel at whatever they do, they don't easily settle for second place. And this is precisely why people all over the world have acknowledged the fact that a Ranger is "a more elite soldier."

This desire to go above and beyond—this avoidance of the average—is seen in other parts of a Ranger's life, too. For example, Rangers typically lead the way in sports and the civilian sector. Motorcycle racing, skydiving, and other high-adrenaline extreme sports are normal for Rangers on any given weekend—along with the rough and tumble injuries that accompany those activities! And when you ask a Ranger what he wants to do with the rest of his life (that is, if he's not planning on staying in the Army for 30 years), you'll hear plans regarding things like the CIA, SWAT, or various academic pursuits such as law school, medical school, and the like.

As you might guess, there's a Ranger ethos that transcends job description, paycheck, and even the highly-coveted emblem worn on a uniform, the black-and-gold Ranger Tab. In other words, being a Ranger is a way of life that fundamentally encompasses every aspect of one's being—it's an identity, not an occupational specialty. At the end of the day, the word "Ranger" doesn't ultimately describe what a man does; rather, it describes who he is.

Every Ranger draws his identity from the words of the Ranger Creed, first codified in 1974 by Command Sergeant Major Neal Gentry but alive in the hearts of Rangers since before the birth of the United States itself. Every Ranger memorizes the Creed, internalizes the Creed, and lives the Creed. Or, as retired General Stanley McChrystal has written, "Although it has a rhythmic quality, the Ranger Creed is neither a poem nor a mindless mantra chanted by the masses. It is a promise, a solemn vow made by each Ranger to every other

Ranger."[1] And when Rangers gather to recite the Creed in unison, thunder electrifies the air and rattles bystanders fortunate enough to hear it. Oftentimes, Rangers recite the Creed before morning physical training and significant unit ceremonies. But Rangers have also recited the Creed in other contexts, whether in an airplane minutes away from jumping into combat in Panama or at the bedside of a seriously-wounded Ranger buddy at Walter Reed National Medical Center. Regardless of the setting, imagine if you will hundreds of men gathered and, with one voice, shouting the following words in unison:

R ecognizing that I volunteered as a Ranger, fully knowing the hazards of my chosen profession, I will always endeavor to uphold the prestige, honor, and high esprit de corps of my Ranger Regiment.

A cknowledging the fact that a Ranger is a more elite soldier, who arrives at the cutting edge of battle by land, sea, or air, I accept the fact that as a Ranger, my country expects me to move further, faster, and fight harder than any other soldier.

N ever shall I fail my comrades. I will always keep myself mentally alert, physically strong, and morally straight, and I will shoulder more than my share of the task, whatever it may be, one hundred percent and then some.

G allantly will I show the world that I am a specially selected and well trained soldier. My courtesy to superior officers, neatness of dress, and care of equipment shall set the example for others to follow.

E nergetically will I meet the enemies of my country. I shall defeat them on the field of battle for I am better trained and will fight with all my might. Surrender is not a Ranger word. I will never leave a fallen comrade to fall into the hands of the enemy and under no circumstances will I ever embarrass my country.

R eadily will I display the intestinal fortitude required to fight on to the Ranger objective and complete the mission, though I be the lone survivor.

Rangers Lead the Way!

The Creed and the Ranger way of life represent the absolute pinnacle of military discipline, esprit de corps, and devotion to defending the United States of America and energetically defeating our Nation's enemies. As a result, the President and people of the United States know that they can enthusiastically depend on Army Rangers to accomplish the toughest missions. Maybe that's why many have used the slogan from the old FedEx television ads when referring to these men: "When it absolutely, positively has to be destroyed overnight, call the Army Rangers!"

A More Elite Man

Yes, America has and will continue to depend on its Rangers to show up at the right place and right time to get the job done. Our Nation has never had to wonder if its Rangers are up to the challenge, whatever it might be. And that's a great example for anyone to follow.

Especially American men.

Perhaps you've noticed that our Nation is in trouble. Statistics leap from the pages of magazines, websites, and newspapers every day that point to the fraying social and moral fabric of the United States. It seems that we've cast off from our time-honored cultural moorings, and now we're drifting without sail or rudder. Worst of all, these statistics hit men at the very points which mean the most—namely, marriages, relationships with children, careers, and even a sense of meaning, purpose, and worth. For example, the homes in which boys become men are often ill equipped to produce a mature product. Today, nearly 35% of all babies are born into homes without fathers (compared to only 3% in 1940). Data shows that fatherless boys are five times more likely to grow up in poverty, repeat grades in school, and develop emotional and mental difficulties. Moreover, 85% of all men in prison come from fatherless homes. Then, once a young man enters the world as an adult—fatherless or not—the challenges only increase. For married men, a whole host of temptations seek to defeat their ability to make, maintain, and honor their commitments to their wives. After all, men are over 500% more likely than women to view pornography and become addicted. Recently some 31 million men got caught with their hands in the Ashley Madison cookie jar—that was the website with the motto, "Life is Short. Have an Affair." Granted, not all of these men hooked up, but clearly they were surfing in those waters for a reason. And sadly, the divorce rate still hovers around the 40% mark for all marriages. Then the cycle begins all over again for a new generation: two years after a divorce, only 53% of the children see their non-custodial parent at least once per month—and the vast majority of non-custodial parents are men.

It's easy to see that the lowest common denominator for many of these alarming statistics is the heartbreaking absence of men—that is, the inability of many men simply to show up and get the job done relationally, personally, and professionally.

This epidemic of American men missing in action isn't new or novel. Rather, we're simply seeing a trajectory play out that began at least a century ago. Since then, generations of American men have checked out, given up, and fallen down. And the rest of the Nation is reaping the harvest of broken homes, broken relationships, and broken lives.

So what's the solution? What's the cure for this epidemic of missing men? Well, the answer is found when men, in spite of the many challenges they face, choose to endeavor and thrive in a cold world where many men are falling by the wayside or barely keeping their heads above water. The answer is found when a man consciously and deliberately chooses to become "a more elite man."

We've already noted that Army Rangers possess a noteworthy purpose, energy, and passion—an ethos—far surpassing that of other soldiers. As a result Rangers demonstrate an uncanny dependability to show up and accomplish any mission. Indeed, a Ranger is "a more elite soldier."

I would argue that when we apply the Army Ranger ethos of purpose, energy, and passion to the quest for manhood, we discover a unique pathway that allows any man to abandon the average and become the man God created him to be—with an emphasis upon the phrase "the man God created him to be." As you will see in chapter one, the Bible above all other voices contains God's plan for the man. It is the external point of reference that leads to relationship and life success. And, time after time, experience and observation show that those men who align themselves with that plan—God's plan—find themselves on life's high ground of peace, righteousness, and legacy.

And that high ground is far above the average.

After all, an average man is happy to get by and survive, but a more elite man desires to thrive. An average man leads from a position of ambiguity—if he leads at all—but a more elite man boldly leads his family and those in his sphere with a confident influence. An average man struggles with dark thoughts and temptations that often lead to emotional and moral failure, but a more elite man becomes master of his emotion and rules his spirit through the power of God.

The concise title of this book, *A More Elite Man*, describes our intent to help men everywhere discover what it means to leave behind an average existence and to become God's man—a more elite man. That quest, wrapped up in the Army Ranger ethos, is not an easy quest. In fact, I would compare it to climbing Mount Everest: it's a challenging climb that intimidates and takes determined effort. But for those who make it to the top, the view is unbelievable!

Our Task and Purpose

Every Ranger has a task and a purpose—that is, they know what they're doing and why they're doing it. We've already laid out our task and purpose above, but it's important to further explain the "why" of this book. After all, others have already said and written much about contemporary manhood according to the Bible. In fact, bookstore shelves are filled with volumes dedicated to helping men succeed. Do we really need another book on this subject?

That's a great question, so let's consider a few constructive answers. First of all, it's important to note that most books about manhood have a lot in common. We might even say that the majority of these books are fundamentally the same and only superficially different—that is, regardless of the author, title, or publisher, there's a good bit of overlap in content. For example, the classic book on Christian manhood, *The Man in the Mirror*, written by Patrick Morley, contains several key themes to include:

1. Purpose: Why Do I Exist?
2. Wives: How to Be a Happily Married Man
3. Children: How to Avoid Regrets
4. Money: The Four Pillars of Financial Strength
5. Priorities: How to Decide What's Important[2]

Another significant book on manhood is *Point Man*. Written by Steve Farrar, it covers a broad array of topics such as:

1. Point Man on Patrol
2. A One-Woman Kind of Man

3. Husband and Wife Teamwork
4. How to Raise Masculine Sons and Feminine Daughters
5. Telling Your Kids What You Don't Want to Tell Them[3]

A hidden gem for men is *The Resolution for Men*. Written by Stephen and Alex Kendrick, it also covers a broadly fundamental scope of topics such as:

1. Resolve to Lead Your Family
2. Resolve to Love Your Wife
3. Resolve to Bless Your Children
4. A Lifelong Vision of Fatherhood
5. Resolve to Live with Integrity[4]

These are just three examples, but even among them you can see some general themes repeated. And, without surprise, you will find many of these themes contained in this book, too.

By the way, this thematic commonality among books on Godly manhood is good news for men everywhere, not least because it shows that the keys to thriving as a man are not mysterious secrets available only to a select few. If that were the case, then the same principles wouldn't appear over and over again in such a wide array of books and resources. This is good news because it dispels the fatalistic assumption that says, "I see a lot of husbands, fathers, and other men stumbling today, so I guess I don't stand a chance, either." Nothing could be further from the truth! Moreover, the fact that the content of this book, in many ways, overlaps with rudimentary themes found in other guidebooks for manhood simply reinforces the idea that the keys to becoming a more elite man are accessible to men everywhere.

On the other hand, there are differences from book to book typically found in the presentation and theme. This is important to note, because different themes and presentations will appeal to different readers. And that's where *A More Elite Man* finds itself in a small yet highly-appealing category. Previously, a handful of authors have applied the Ranger theme to spirituality and faith with an application for men—for example, *A More Elite Soldier* by Chuck Holton, *The Road to Unafraid* by Jeff Struecker, and *Jesus Was an Airborne Ranger* by John McDougall.[5] These books, written largely from a biographical perspective by Rangers who have "been there and done that," weave spiritual concepts throughout the narrative. While sharing some commonalities with those volumes, *A More Elite Man* focuses directly, topically, and practically on challenges that men face in twenty-first century America. Couched in Ranger verbiage and concepts while still accessible and appealing to a broader audience, this book presents a fresh perspective on becoming God's man.

For men serving in the military, the application is obvious and the need is urgent. More than fifteen years of persistent conflict in this Global War on Terror have spread heavy burdens upon men serving in all branches of the service, and a word about going the distance and finishing well as a warrior, husband, and father will be a welcome encouragement. But the general population of men, regardless of their background, will also find the book informative and engaging. For one thing, the spotlight on Army Rangers and other special operations soldiers has never been brighter, and public attention toward these men has never been greater. In light of this interest, many men will eagerly read *A More Elite Man* with a curiosity about the Ranger culture. But along the way, they will learn how men can apply Ranger principles to their own quest to become God's more elite man.

Each chapter borrows from the Ranger culture, the Ranger Creed, and other aspects of Ranger life and applies those principles to the quest for Godly manhood. Overall, the book is divided into two parts followed by a final chapter that closes the book.

The first part, chapters one through six, addresses the disciplines of a more elite man. Chapter One, "Life Navigation: Finding Your Way to God's High Ground," encourages men to honestly assess themselves in light of God's definition of life and relationship success. This chapter, with its use of navigational imagery and emphasis upon the themes of "vision" and "decision," sets the stage for the rest of the book. Men will finish this chapter with a crystal clear picture of God's map to life's high ground. Chapter Two, "Discipline: Self Leadership Precedes Team Leadership," highlights one of the greatest challenges that men have faced since the dawn of time, and the message to men is clear: you cannot lead others unless you first take charge of yourself. Chapter Three, "Team Leadership: A Man's Highest Calling," helps men to cultivate a vision for influence and leadership in their immediate spheres and beyond. The battlecry "Rangers Lead the Way," first uttered on the D-Day beaches in 1944, provides today's man with a dynamic leadership paradigm. Chapter Four, "I Will Always Endeavor: Fear God and Take Your Own Part," focuses on the balance between Ranger hustle and personal faith to illustrate the fundamentals of life success according to God's economy. Chapter Five, "My Care of Equipment: Financial Wisdom in a Foolish World," provides men with perspectives and skills for mastering their money and possessions rather than being mastered by them. Chapter Six, "Spiritual Athlete Warrior: Personal Training In God's Gym," uses the Ranger's commitment to the physical gym as an example of a more elite man's commitment to spending time in the spiritual gym.

The second part, chapters seven through nine, addresses the key relationships of a more elite man. Chapter Seven, "Your Dad's Leadership: His Influence and Impact," deals with perhaps the most fundamental topic for manhood: the relationship men have with their fathers. Good, bad, ugly, or non-existent, each man simply must understand how this key relationship impacts his own quest to become God's more elite man. Chapter Eight, "Give Way Together:

The Commander's Intent for Marriage," encourages men to view their marriage relationship through the lens of the Bible and bring the Ranger's purpose and energy to the most important earthly relationship a man will ever experience. Chapter Nine, "Fathers Lead the Way: Developing Influence With Your Kids," helps men to understanding and engage in life's greatest leadership and legacy-leaving opportunity—the role of being a dad.

The last chapter, "How to Get a GO with God: The Greatest Question a Man Will Ever Answer," highlights in Ranger terminology the greatest and most pressing aspect of being a more elite man—the relationship that we receive with God through the life, death, and resurrection of Jesus Christ. Every man must ultimately answer the question, "What will I do with Jesus?" This chapter helps every man answer that question.

1
Life Navigation: Finding Your Way to God's High Ground

The roots of the term "Ranger" stretch back hundreds of years to the days when colonial soldiers in North America moved long distances over unknown, challenging, and oftentimes hostile terrain. For example, in 1622 Captain John Smith led over 100 soldiers on an expedition through uncharted colonial territory, writing afterward, "When I had the men, I ranged that unknown country 14 weeks." Likewise, in 1637 during war with the Pequot Indians, John Winthrop wrote that he and his men spent their time "ranging up and down the countryside."[1] For more than 300 years since then, whether moving across the frontier searching for French and Indians or patrolling long distances in the Vietnamese jungles to close with and destroy the Communists, Rangers have demonstrated a keen ability to move across unknown and hostile terrain in order to reach their objective. Indeed, to this day, the quintessential Ranger operation includes walking a long distance, overcoming obstacles and challenges along the way, and arriving at an objective to execute a mission. For Rangers throughout the centuries, very little has changed in this regard.

Rangers prize their ability to navigate across broad, unknown expanses so much that land navigation is one of the first and most critical skills tested during the 62-day U. S. Army Ranger School conducted at Fort Benning, Georgia. Given a compass and map of the training area, the student receives a list of grid coordinates. His task is to plot those coordinates on the map and then navigate to those points. A marker with certain numbers is located at each point, and the student must find the marker, write down the number, then move to his next point. Ultimately, he must find all of the points and return to the starting point within a certain amount of time. And did I mention that over half of the time allotted is during morning darkness? It's a challenge! But the challenge is not over once a student passes the land navigation test. Rather, he must still demonstrate proficiency throughout the two-month course while conducting numerous missions with his squad and platoon. Simply put, if a student cannot navigate through the woods and find his objective, he will never be a Ranger.

For a Ranger, there's no worse feeling that realizing that you've lost your way in the woods. How do I know? Well, when I went to Ranger School I failed my first attempt at the land navigation test. I started off well enough and found several points in the dark. But then I began to run in circles and crisscrossed the training area in search of more points. I began to see the same intersections and locations over and over again. As time began to run out, I had to admit that I was disoriented. Fortunately, I passed my retest a few days later and continued with training, but I've never forgotten what it felt like to feel desperate and lost in the woods.

Life Navigation

Most men today could take a page from the Ranger playbook on land navigation, couldn't they? After all, men have the challenging task of discovering and determining their objective in life and then coming up with a way to reach that objective. For men, life itself is often filled with unknown and challenging terrain. The task is to navigate successfully through all of that and arrive at the "high ground" of relationship and life success. Sadly, many men today are aimlessly wandering around the woods of life with neither a plan nor an objective. Whether they're simply living for the moment or pursuing something that ultimately won't satisfy in the long run, a large number of today's men are disoriented and lost in the woods of life.

I would argue that every man needs to understand the concept of "life navigation"—that is, understand the process of defining and identifying their life's objective and then developing a clear plan for navigating to it. Or in other words, I like to talk about a man's "vision" (a picture of where he wants his life to go in the long run) and his "decision" (his plan for getting there). These are powerful words for any man, and the Ranger model of land navigation can play a big role in assisting him to find life's high ground.

Vision: Guidance from Higher

Every Ranger mission begins with guidance from higher headquarters. That is to say, Rangers don't just pull their mission's objective out of thin air. The commanding officer tells the Ranger where he is to go and generally what he is to do when he arrives. The Ranger's job is to (1) understand that objective and (2) come up with the plan for getting there and the details of what to do upon arrival.

One of the fundamentals of being a more elite man is to honestly seek guidance from higher headquarters regarding your objective— that is, your life's vision. In other words, a more elite man needs to look to God for his life's vision, direction, and objective rather than pulling it out of thin air. The man who does this will be truly blessed. On the other hand, when a man tries to find his way in life apart from God, he does so at his own peril and normally ends up disoriented and lost in the woods of life.

This concept of life navigation is nothing new. Men have been trying to guide themselves without God's guidance since ancient times and have been failing miserably at life navigation ever since. For example, consider this Bible verse: "In those days . . . everyone did what seemed right in his own eyes" (Judges 21:25). In other words, the men were trying to do life navigation with nothing more than their own internal sense of guidance. And what did that produce? Well, if you were to skim the pages of the book of Judges, you'd see that the culture of that day was eaten up with things like disobedience to God, idolatry, greedy materialism, rampant sexual immorality, corrupt religious leaders, robbery, gang rape, and kidnapping. (Sounds a lot like twenty-first century America, doesn't it?) Yes, the entire culture of that day was totally lost in the woods of life! But that shouldn't surprise us. After all, think about what Proverbs 14:12 tells us: "There is a way which seems right to a man, but its end leads to destruction."

So what does it look like to receive your guidance and vision from higher headquarters? Consider this powerful passage from the Bible:

> *Whether you turn to the right or to the left, your ears will hear a voice behind you saying, "This is the way, walk in it. . . . I am the Lord your God, who teaches you what is best for you, who directs you in the way you should go [so that] your peace would be like a river, your righteousness like the waves of the sea, your descendants like the sand, and your children like its numberless grains; their name would never be cut off or destroyed before me."* (Isaiah 30:21; 48:17, 19)

Take a minute to consider what God promises in this passage. First and foremost, he promises to guide us toward what is "best." You know, there's a lot of chatter in our world today about what we should do, how we should live, and where we should go. Everybody wants to give us their opinion on life, happiness, and prosperity. But who's to say what's really best? I believe it's safe to say that God is probably the only voice fully qualified to tell us what's best. After all, he has unlimited insight into our past, present, future, and our very being. He also understands better than anyone the full value of life and relationship success. That's probably why he identifies things like peace, righteousness, and legacy (i.e., descendants and children—in short, family) as the goals that every man should seek and treasure. In fact, we might even say that those are the grid-points on God's high ground for every man: peace, righteousness, and legacy.

So what exactly are peace, righteousness, and legacy? In a nutshell, peace and righteousness refer to a healthy relationship with God and healthy relationships with those around us. This concept is best illustrated in Bible passages such as Matthew 22:37-40, where Jesus answered a question about which commandment was the greatest. He said:

> *You shall love the Lord your God with all your heart and with all your soul and with all your mind. This is the great and first commandment. And a second is like it: You shall love your neighbor as yourself. All of the Law and the Prophets hang on these two commandments.*

A right relationship with God begins through Jesus Christ, who died that every man might have his sins forgiven and receive a new, everlasting life. And the new life that Jesus gives to those who personally receive him allows a man both to love God and to love his neighbor. Apart from Jesus, a man can do neither of lasting significance.

And what is legacy? Legacy is an all-encompassing word that includes the concept of a sound, enduring, and God-centered marriage that produces children and future descendants who love God and walk in his truth. Think about these words from Psalm 128:1-6 and listen to the ongoing blessings of legacy:

> *Blessed is everyone who fears the Lord, who walks in his ways! You shall eat the fruit of the labor of your hands; you shall be blessed, and it shall be well with you. Your wife will be like a fruitful vine within your house; your children will be like olive plants around your table. Behold, thus shall the man be blessed who fears the Lord. May you see the prosperity of Jerusalem all the days of your life! May you see your children's children!*

God has indeed shown us the grid points on his high ground: peace, righteousness, and legacy. But are men navigating toward those things today? Unfortunately, many men are actually going 180 degrees in the opposite direction from peace, righteousness, and legacy. A large number of men today wrestle with misplaced priorities on material possessions and leisure, display unhealthy devotion to their careers, and struggle with things like overwhelming debt, alcohol abuse, pornography addiction, anger, and depression. Yes, some men have experienced circumstances that are simply beyond their control. But most of the time—*most of the time*—they struggle because they have discarded God's guidance. As a result, they are disoriented in the woods of life and are in danger of failing life navigation.

But it doesn't have to be that way, and God never stops offering to lead men toward the blessings of peace, righteousness, and legacy no matter how far they have drifted.

Vision: External Points of Reference

Every Ranger understands the need for external points of reference, even if he hasn't consciously thought about it. In other words, no Ranger in his right mind would try to find his way across unknown terrain at night using nothing but this own internal sense of guidance. Rather, he's going to use some kind of external reference points in order to find his objective. In most cases, those external reference points are tools like a map and a compass; however, a Ranger could even navigate by the sun, moon, and stars. But the point is that if a Ranger relies exclusively upon his "gut instinct" he will end up lost every time.

We spoke a moment ago about "guidance from higher headquarters" and how God wants to lead us toward peace, righteousness, and legacy—the grid points on his high ground. Let's now talk specifically about the external points of reference by which God guides us toward that high ground.

First and foremost, God uses the Bible to speak to us about what is best and how to find our way to peace, righteousness, and legacy. For thousands of years, men have looked to the Bible for guidance and direction—and for good reason, too. It is God's word to every generation. It comes from God and has God's imprint of truth upon every page. Consider this description: "All Scripture is inspired [God-breathed] and is useful for teaching, rebuking, correcting, and training in righteousness" (2 Timothy 3:16). Or how about these words describing the Bible's impeccable quality: "The words of the Lord are flawless, like silver refined in a furnace of clay, purified seven times" (Psalm 12:6). Like a map that has been verified or a compass that has been perfectly calibrated, the Bible provides men everywhere with God's pathway to life's high ground. Thus, throughout this book, we will reference the Bible for guidance and direction for becoming God's more elite man.

We might also mention another external point of reference that every man must have in his life, and that point of reference is the voice of another man of character, wisdom, and faith. This is a critical part of life navigation, and I cannot say it strongly or loudly enough when I say that no man will find his way to God's high ground without at least one other man of truth and integrity walking alongside him and encouraging him along the way. And this is precisely where many men are drifting. Or as Stephen Arterburn puts it in his fantastic book *Every Young Man, God's Man*: "The number-one dilemma facing God's young men today is not all sorts of sexual or material temptation. It's isolation."[2] We as men have many associates, many co-workers, and many neighbors up and down the street, but how many true friends of faith and wisdom do we have speaking God's truth and encouragement into our lives on a regular basis? For most men, the answer is "none." That's why verses like these from the Bible are so important for life navigation:

As iron sharpens iron, so one man sharpens his friend. (Proverbs 27:17)

Encourage each other every day, as long as it is called "Today," so that you may not become ensnared by the deceitfulness of sin. (Hebrews 3:13)

Let us not give up meeting together . . . but let us encourage one another—and all the more as you see the day [of Christ's return] approaching. (Hebrews 10:25)

We'll have a lot more to say about this concept later, but for now let's simply agree that we need voices of wisdom, truth, character, and integrity in our lives if we're ever going to become God's more elite man.

By the way, while we're talking about external points of reference, let's consider an important aspect of land navigation that readily applies to life navigation. I'm talking about what's called an "azimuth check." When a Ranger conducts land navigation, he plots the points on his map and determines the direction he must walk to those points. That direction is called an azimuth, and it's normally measured in degrees on a compass—for example, 34 degrees, 128 degrees, 251 degrees, and so forth. And when he's ready to take his first step toward his first point, he puts his compass up to his eye, makes sure that he's pointed toward the right azimuth, and then he starts walking. Typically, that first point will be anywhere from 500 to 800 meters away. After he's walked around 30 to 50 meters, a smart Ranger will stop, put the compass up to his eye once again, and reconfirm that he's still walking along the same azimuth. That's called an azimuth check. And the more frequently a Ranger conducts an azimuth check, the more likely he will maintain his proper heading and, ultimately, find his desired point. Conversely, the Ranger who rarely ever stops and conducts an azimuth check will invariably drift to the left or the right and ultimately miss his point altogether. Or as a Ranger School Instructor once said, "The student who is slave to his compass can confidently move forward; the careless student who neglects his compass will never find his points . . . and will NEVER be a Ranger."

The application of this principle to life navigation is all too easy. Those men who make frequent "azimuth checks" with the external points of reference that God supplies—namely, the Bible and the voices of men of character and faith—will very likely arrive at God's high ground of peace, righteousness, and legacy. In other words, every time a man opens his Bible to read it, every time he attends church, and every time he comes to a Bible study, it's as if he's putting a compass up to his eye to reconfirm that his life is heading in the right direction. And every time a man touches base with another man of truth and wisdom, it's as if he's rechecking his azimuth to ensure that he's not drifting away from God's direction and plan. On the other hand, the man who neglects his Bible and neglects to build relationships with the right kind of men will doubtlessly drift away from God's azimuth for his life.

Vision: Determine Your Purpose

We've talked so far about some broad life navigation principles such as vision, external points of reference, and getting your guidance from higher. Now it's time to get specific as you personally begin to think about your own life's vision and objective. In other words, what is God telling you about what your life should look like down the road? Yes, we've touched upon the broad concepts of peace, righteousness, and legacy, and we would all agree that those are important. But what exactly will those look like in YOUR life?

A good place to start is Stephen Covey's book *Seven Habits of Highly Effective People*, especially the second habit: "Begin with the end in mind."[3] This is a serious challenge for men today, largely because most men are not thinking about the big picture—rather, they're living for the moment and the pleasures that moment can provide without considering the long-term impacts of their decisions. But a more elite man will live his life and make decisions today that set him up to enjoy God's blessings of peace, righteousness, and legacy years from now. Or, as Psalm 90:12 says, "Teach us to number our days, that we may gain a heart of wisdom."

When thinking about the big picture and the long look on life, every man must determine what his life's purpose is and then align his life with that purpose. We might define purpose as vision and objective distilled down into individual terms for an individual man. In other words, the purpose for your life is God's vision and objective "with your name on it." As we've already mentioned, things like peace, righteousness, and legacy apply to all men everywhere, but each man must determine how those apply to his life personally.

Few men have taken the time to think this deeply about God's purpose for their lives. But those who home in on that purpose tap into a unique source of energy and power. As James Loehr and Tony Schwartz have written in *The Power of Full Engagement*, "A fierce and compelling sense of purpose . . . fuels focus, direction, passion, and perseverance."[4] After all, it's one thing to think about God's broad intent for mankind; it's something altogether different when a man applies that purpose to himself personally.

So how does a man discover and apply God's purpose for his life? It's a three-step process whereby a man (1) considers how God's purpose might apply to his life, (2) organizes that purpose in a concise manner, and (3) writes it down. Let's do that now.

By the way, it should be obvious that God's purpose for every man revolves primarily around relationships—relationships with God, relationships with others, and relationships with families. This may sound surprising given that our culture seems to prioritize achievement, accumulation of possessions, and activities that provide personal pleasure and fulfillment. Yet at the end of the day—*at the end of life*—all that will really matter are relationships found in peace, righteousness, and legacy. Therefore, as a man considers God's purpose for his life and writes it down, he should keep in mind that whatever he writes down should be centered primarily in relationships.

Michael Hyatt, in his book *Living Forward*, suggests that discovering God's purpose for your life begins with listing your key relationships: God, spouse, children, parents, siblings, colleagues, friends, those you have mentored, etc.[5] Then describe how you want to be remembered by each key person. Yes, we're basically asking you to write what you would want them to say about you after you're gone from this earth.

This little exercise helps us as men to narrow our focus and prioritize what really matters the most to us. To be sure, much of what we pursue in life doesn't matter all that much when compared to what echoes through eternity after we're gone. Next, Hyatt suggests that you actually write your own eulogy—that is, sum up what you would want someone who knew you best to say about you at your funeral. Again, this helps us to separate those things that really matter most—peace, righteousness, and legacy—from those things that, while seemingly important now, would sound ridiculous during an actual eulogy that summarizes our life's purpose and work. For example, statements such as, "John was a rabid college football fan and he lived for Saturday afternoons in the fall" or "Steve lived to hunt deer and shoot ducks—that was his passion in life," sound shallow and superficial as summations of a man's life. One would hope to be remembered for more substantive contributions to the lives of others. But at the end of the day, your eulogy is just that . . . YOUR eulogy. Choose whatever words you like so long as you choose them carefully.

I have taken Hyatt's advice and have drafted a eulogy of my own. May I share it with you as an example?

After a life-changing experience with Christ at age seventeen, Phil spent a lifetime making God his priority and Jesus his Lord. At the top of his life's list, he relentlessly pursued God's vision for a Christ-centered family, first by preparing himself as a man, then by marrying his best friend and spiritual soul-mate, Shara. Together, they determined that their relationship and family should be a shining city on a hill that would encourage and help others to find God's best. Together, they raised five children with the priority that says, "I have no greater joy than to know that my children walk in the truth." Phil energetically loved and invested in his children as a means to cultivate spiritual and emotional influence with them. As a man, Phil believed that "a man can receive nothing unless it has been given to him from Heaven" while also believing that "the plans of the diligent lead surely to plenty." As a result, he sought to "walk by faith" while also pursuing excellence at all times and in all things. He earned numerous academic degrees, to include the Doctor of Philosophy. He served 20 years in the military, both as an enlisted Marine with service at the Presidential Retreat at Camp David and also as an Army Chaplain for Airborne Rangers and Paratroopers with multiple tours in Afghanistan and Iraq. He subsequently served 20 years as a pastor. All along the way, Phil diligently sought to lead, encourage, and influence others to experience the life and blessings that come through faith in the Word of God and obedience to the Son of God.

Maybe you've never thought about summing up your life in such a way—yours might be longer than mine; it might be shorter. It's a very helpful exercise that assists in highlighting what is most important and also putting in a proper light those frivolous things that probably get too much of our time and resources now. And by the way, once you've written your eulogy, share it with a few trusted people who know you best and ask, "Does this at all represent how I'm actually living my life now?"

After writing your eulogy, distill what you have written into a 3-5 sentence paragraph beginning with the phrase, "The purpose of my life" or "My life's purpose is." Again, as an example, let me share with you my life's purpose statement:

The purpose of my life is to love God and follow his Son, Jesus Christ. I want to love my wife and invest in my children so that our family would reflect God's glory. I want to trust God at all times and always endeavor to give my best to any task at hand. I want to lead and influence others to believe God's Word and to follow his Son.

After writing a concise purpose statement for your life, conduct a brief litmus test by asking yourself, "Does this purpose line up with God's purpose of peace, righteousness, and legacy?" Also, as mentioned above, ask a few of your close family members or friends, "Does this purpose statement reflect how I am living my life now?"

Once a man identifies and captures God's purpose for his life in writing, he has a pretty good picture of God's high ground for his life—he has the exact grid coordinates for where he needs to go. And then it's time for a decision on how to get there. It's time to start navigating.

Decision: Route Selection

Once a Ranger knows his objective, he must select a route for getting there. That might sound easy, since an old adage says, "The shortest distance between two points is a straight line." So the quick-thinking Ranger might simply draw a straight line between his current location and his objective and then start walking. But much more goes into route selection than drawing a straight line. For example, a Ranger must consider which terrain will best facilitate his movement as well as which terrain is impassible (such as a water obstacle or a high cliff) and which terrain lacks cover and concealment (such as a large open field). Additionally, a Ranger must consider known and suspected enemy locations. In other words, route selection chooses those things that will aid in land navigation and avoids those things that will hinder it. And the Ranger who disregards the difference is only asking for trouble.

Route selection in life navigation is all about decisions, and it's important to understand the significance of the decisions we make as men—after all, life is a sum total of the decisions we make. Or, as Adrian Rogers often said, "Your decisions determine your destiny." Of course, we are free to choose. But once we choose, we are not free to choose the consequences of those choices. And sooner or later, as Robert Louis Stevenson reportedly said, "Every man must eventually sit down to a banquet of consequences." It's the ancient principle of sowing and reaping: "Do not be deceived, God is not mocked. Whatever a man sows, that shall he also reap" (Galatians 6:7).

The bottom line is that there's only one way to navigate to God's high grounds of peace, righteousness, and legacy: over the course of your life, you must make a series of wise decisions guided by God. And those decisions will determine your destiny. That's certainly the truth found in Deuteronomy 30:15-19 where God says:

> *I have set before you life and good, death and evil. If you obey the commandments of the Lord your God by walking in his ways, then you shall live and multiply, and the Lord your God will bless you. But if your heart turns away and are drawn to worship other gods and serve them, you shall surely perish. I call heaven and earth to witness against you today, that I have set before you life and death, blessings and curse. Therefore, choose life, that you and your offspring may life.*

Beware of Functional Atheism

As you select a route for your life, it's important to deliberately keep God right in the middle of your decision-making. One of the most common mistakes when men plan for the future is that they forget all about God in the first place. It's not that they don't believe in God or that they are out and out against him. Rather, they just go ahead with their plans without really thinking at all about what he might want—about what his purpose might be and how to pursue it. When that happens, a man is in danger of committing what I call "functional atheism."

"And what," you might ask, "is functional atheism?" Well, let's unpack the definition. What is an atheist? It's someone who says, "There is no God." Now, if you're a "functional" anything, then you're functioning along the lines specified. So a functional atheist, essentially, is someone who functions as one who says, "There is no God." And when, from the beginning, you make all of your plans for life without taking God's desires and purposes into consideration, you're basically functioning as one who doesn't believe that God exists. That's not to say that you don't, in fact, believe in God. It just means that you're acting like you don't.

Let's look at the story of a man who did that very thing:

> *Jesus told them this parable: "The ground of a certain rich man produced a good crop. He thought to himself, 'What shall I do? I have no place to store my crops.' Then he said, This is what I will do. I will tear down my barns and build bigger barns, and there I will store my grain and my goods. And I'll say to myself, "You have plenty of good things laid up for many years. Take life easy; eat, drink, and be merry.'" But God said to him, 'You fool! This very night your life will be demanded from you. Then who will get what you have prepared for yourself?' This is how it will be with anyone who stores up things for himself but is not rich toward God."* (Luke 12:16-21)

Evidently, this man was a very gifted businessman and farmer. He had a bumper crop and he knew how to multiply his wealth—and there's nothing wrong with any of that, per se. But where was God in his plans? To some degree, I'm certain he was a religious man. But in the day-to- day operation of his business, why didn't he make God his business partner . . . or, better yet, his boss? It's not surprising that God came to him and called him a "fool." Of course, God could have called him just about anything—for example, "knucklehead," "clown," or "idiot." But it's very significant that he calls him a "fool," because that's the word in the Old Testament for someone who says there is no God. (Psalm 14:1 says, "The fool has said in his heart, 'There is no God.'")

So, as you plan your route, don't forget to take God's purpose into consideration. Otherwise, you might end up with egg on your face at the end of the day.

Criteria for Route Selection

When selecting a route, every man must ask himself this question: "Will this decision take me closer to my objective or further from it?" That's why your purpose statement is so important—it's the anchor for every decision you make. Certainly there are other questions that you can ask as criteria for your route selection, but they must always be tied in some way to your purpose statement. For me and my life's purpose statement, every decision I make must answer one of these questions:

1. Will this decision help me to love God more and follow him better? Or will it take me further away from God?
2. Will this decision make me a better husband and father?
3. Will this decision help me to lead and influence others to love and follow God?

What are some other examples of criteria for making wise decisions? One example is the "10-10-10 principle." Not long ago, Suzy Welch wrote a wildly-popular book entitled *10-10-10: A Life Transforming Idea*. In the book, she highlights some decision-making criteria worth considering: "Are our decisions the right ones? Or are we being governed time and again by the demands of the moment?" Basically, she challenges everyone to ask three questions about every decision they're about to make. First, "What will be the effects of this decision 10 minutes after I've made it?" Second, "What will be the effects of this decision 10 months after I've made it?" And third, "What will be the effects of this decision 10 years after I've made it?"[6]

Another set of questions comes from Chicago-area pastor James MacDonald. In a message entitled "Decision Time," he listed seven criteria he uses for making near-term and long-term decisions.[7] Again, like the 10-10-10 principle, this is a very practical way to weed out bad choices that you're thinking about making and highlighting those choices that are best. Here they are:

1. Will this decision bring glory to God?
2. Would Jesus make this decision (or at least not criticize it)?
3. Will I be proud of this decision when I someday stand before God?
4. How will this decision affect my faith in God?
5. How will this decision affect my family—my wife and my children (or my future wife and children)?
6. How will this decision affect prior commitments?
7. Can I financially afford this decision?

The great thing about James MacDonald's list is that it's deeply spiritual but also intensely practical. On the one hand, it takes into consideration the deeper questions of life—that is, it puts the decision-making process squarely in the sphere of God's economy and desires. Additionally, it takes the big picture into perspective, which is to say that it reminds us that life isn't just about *right now*. On the other hand, it touches upon some of the more temporal issues that every man must address: relationships, commitments, money, and so forth. In that regard, it's a pretty comprehensive list.

Both the 10-10-10 principle and James MacDonald's list are helpful for route selection in that both encourage men to consider the big picture. As men, we often focus only on the immediate without asking ourselves about the long-reaching impacts of our choices. The key application for life navigation is that men would do well to consider whether or not their decisions are contributing to their arrival at God's high ground and purpose for their lives.

Decision: Terrain Association

Once a Ranger has plotted and chosen his route, it's time to start walking. He puts one foot in front of the other and begins his movement. As we've already noted, he will pause occasionally to lift his compass up to his eye for an azimuth check. This will ensure that he's still heading in the right direction. And the more frequently he does this, the more likely he'll stay on course.

There's another key technique that helps a Ranger to maintain awareness of his location and accurately find his objective. It's called "terrain association." In a nutshell, terrain association concerns the relationship between what a Ranger sees on his map and the terrain he sees before him. It's a really simple concept for confirming the Ranger's location, especially to affirm if he's in the right place. Basically, the Ranger looks at his map and determines his location— or at least where he *thinks* he is! Then he looks at the terrain to his front. If the terrain that he sees matches the terrain depicted on the map (a hill, ridge, slope, water feature, or ravine, for example), then he knows he's in the right place. On the other hand, if the Ranger sees one thing on his map but something entirely different to his front, then he knows that he's not in the right place.

How does this apply to life navigation? Simply put, you look at your map (the Bible) and see what it has to say about believing a certain thing or living a certain way, and then you look at your life and the decisions you're making and see if they match what the Bible has to say. And what can you conclude by doing that? Well, if your life looks a lot like what you see in the Bible, then you're on the right track. But if your life doesn't look at all like what you see in the Bible, then you've got a problem—that is, you've drifted from your azimuth and need to get back on track.

Let's illustrate this principle with just a few examples.

Major Phil Kramer

Emotional Terrain Association

While women are usually known as the emotional half of the human race, men also have emotions—and Rangers are no exception. Of course, being type-A, competitive, strong males, Rangers have some predictable emotions. For example, Rangers are not immune to the emotion of anger. In fact, someone has pointed out that "you can't spell 'Ranger' without A-N-G-E-R." After all, Rangers operate in a high-stress environment where much is demanded of them. Moreover, Ranger leaders are expected to coach, teach, and mentor their junior Rangers with an iron hand. ("Rangers learn through pain and repetition," a platoon sergeant once told me.) But one of the second-order effects of operating in this environment is an angry disposition. While some Rangers are pretty easy going, others live only a few steps away from anger at any given moment. And it's not just Rangers who struggle with anger. Consider Keith Walendowski from Milwaukee, Wisconsin. He might have been a former Ranger—I'm not sure—but, believe it or not, he *shot* his lawnmower. According to the criminal complaint, Walendowski said he was angry because his lawnmower wouldn't start. Now he faces up to $11,000 in fines and six years in prison.[8] Sounds like he needs some anger management, right?

So how does terrain association work when it comes to a man and his emotions—in this case, anger? First, let's look at the map and see what it says about anger. James 1:19-20 says, "Everyone should be quick to listen, slow to speak, and slow to become angry; for the anger of man does not produce the righteousness of God." And let's not forget that Proverbs 16:31 says, "He who is slow to become angry is better than a mighty man, and he who has self-control is better than he who captures a city." In a nutshell, then, the map says that a man should have control over his anger if he's ever going to find his way to peace, righteousness, and legacy. Next, a man must look seriously at his own life and do some "terrain association." If he sees an ability to control his anger, then he's in the right place. But if he has anger issues, then he's not in the right place and he needs to make a course correction if he's ever going to find peace, righteousness, and legacy.

Moral Terrain Association

OK, now let's try another example of terrain association. Let's talk about the moral aspect of this process. After all, Rangers have vowed in the Ranger Creed to be "morally straight," right? So, just as an example, let's see what the map says about the way a man looks at a woman who is not his wife.

First, we see that the map is very clear on this matter. In the Old Testament, we see things like, "I made a covenant with my eyes that I would not look lustfully at a woman" (Job 31:1). And in the New Testament, we see Jesus saying, "I tell you that everyone who looks at a woman with lust for her has already committed sexual immorality with her in his heart" (Matthew 5:28). And Proverbs 6:27-28 takes it one step farther when it talks about the impacts of lust upon a man's heart and soul: "Can a man take fire in his heart and not be burned? Or can a man walk on hot coals and his feet not be burned?" Thus, it's very obvious what the map says: lusting after a woman who is not your wife is a NO-GO. It certainly doesn't set up a man for peace, righteousness, and legacy. Next we should examine our lives in relationship to what we see on the map. If we're not having a problem with lust, porn, and undressing women with our eyes, then we're in the right place. But if any (or all) of these things are filling our lives, then we're not in the right place and we need to get where we ought to be. (By the way, we'll talk more about this in the chapter on discipline and self-leadership.)

Spiritual Terrain Association

OK, one more example of terrain association in a man's life. Let's consider the spiritual dimension, especially the practice of getting together on a consistent basis with other people of faith. After all, the map clearly says, "Let us not give up meeting together, as some are in the habit of doing, but let us encourage one another [by meeting together]" (Hebrews 10:25). Thus, a man should look at his own life to see if he is consistently gathering with other believers in Jesus Christ—that is, is he leading himself and his family to consistently attend and belong to a local church? If so, then he's in the right place. If not, then he's drifting away from God's high ground of peace, righteousness, and legacy.

It's Time to Move Out

Well, we've spent enough time talking about life navigation. Now it's time to apply it to your life. In the coming pages, we're going to discuss numerous topics that will, by God's grace, equip you to find your way to God's high ground of relationship and life success. The man who diligently fixes his eyes upon the goals of peace, righteousness, and legacy will not drift to the left or to the right. Instead, step by step, he will over the course of time, find his way to God's best.

2

Discipline: Self-Leadership Precedes Team-Leadership

In recent years, we've seen some high-level leaders in the United States Army go down in flames legally and morally. Most recently, David Haight, former commander of the 2nd Ranger Battalion, was reduced in rank from Major General to Lieutenant Colonel when details of his decade-long extramarital affair and "swinger" lifestyle caught the attention of the Army's Inspector General. Haight, who most recently directed operations for the Army's European Command, now lives with dishonor and a significant decrease in retirement pay.[1] Only a few years earlier, Jeff Sinclair, former deputy commander of the 82nd Airborne Division and veteran of the 75th Ranger Regiment, was reduced from Brigadier General to Lieutenant Colonel when convicted of adultery and 13 other violations of military law in exchange for dismissal of charges that he sexually assaulted a subordinate female officer. After receiving his sentence, he remorsefully said, "I have squandered a fortune of life's blessings. I don't have to look any further than the mirror for someone to blame. I put myself and the Army in this position with my selfish, self-destructive actions."[2] And then there's David Petraeus, perhaps the most storied General Officer since Norman Schwarzkopf. This wizard of the Iraq counterinsurgency strategy and former CIA director infamously sold his military birthright for a morsel of adulterous pleasure.[3]

These are only three of many examples we could list.

What do these fallen leaders all have in common, these titans of twenty-first century military might? What can be said about the chink in their otherwise impervious armor? First and foremost, although they were in command of thousands of troops, they overlooked the most fundamental principle of leadership—namely, they forgot to lead themselves. Or as Michael Hyatt has written, "Self-leadership precedes team leadership."[4]

To be sure, self-leadership shapes the life of a more elite man as much as any other quality. Without discipline, a man has little hope of relationship and life success on this earth. Without self-control, the values of peace, righteousness, and legacy are little more than vanishing vapors. And on top of that, the man who cannot lead himself will never successfully lead others at home, in his community, or in the professional world.

The Bible places a high premium on self-control and self-leadership. For example, think about these words from the Old Testament:

> *A man who lacks self-control is like a city whose walls are broken down . . . [but] he who rules his spirit is better than one who conquers a city.* (Proverbs 16:32; 25:28)

The illustration is obvious: a man who cannot control himself is like a base camp in enemy territory with no defensive perimeter. He's ripe for the picking and it's only a matter of time before he's overrun. On the other hand, the man who can exercise discipline and self control—a man who understands the self-leadership principle—will have the world at his fingertips and influence over many. On a similar note, consider also this important imperative in the New Testament:

Walk by the Spirit, and you will not gratify the desires of the flesh. [For] the fruit of the Spirit is ... self control. (Galatians 5:16, 22-23)

Over and against the "desires of the flesh" (we'll unpack those in a minute), the fruit of the Spirit brings about results that typify a more elite man, things that demonstrate a man's ability to rule his spirit.

Clearly, a more elite man will demonstrate discipline and self-control in his own life before he ever attempts to lead others. As we have already mentioned, God has called men everywhere to roles of leadership. This chapter discusses the fundamental need for self-control and features several characteristics of self-leadership, all of which equip a man to go forward in life and lead others toward peace, righteousness, and legacy. Following this chapter, we will discuss how a more elite man can take the lead in a broader sense. But first, he must understand and embrace the concept of self-leadership.

Self-Leadership Challenges

We've already touched upon the tragic results that naturally follow reckless self-indulgence. The challenge is real, and men everywhere must understand the reason why discipline and self-control are so vital to the pursuit of peace, righteousness, and legacy. Indeed, the road to self-leadership is littered with obstacles, and every man must consider and overcome them. It's a battle he must fight and win.

In order to better understand the road to self-leadership, let's expand upon the Bible passage from the book of Galatians we mentioned above. When we see the word "flesh" in the Bible, it can either refer to the physical human body or it can refer to that part of every human being that opposes God and everything that's good and right and true. In this case in Galatians, it refers to the latter. (Sometimes people substitute the word "self" when referring to the flesh in this way.) Even in the lives of those who have experienced redemption and forgiveness through Jesus Christ, the flesh still maintains a toe-hold until death and a presence with God in Heaven. There's no way to get around it—every man, woman, boy, and girl is infected with this spiritual and moral cancer called "the flesh." In fact, Jesus Christ was the only person with immunity.

When thinking about the flesh and how it affects men and women, it would be much easier if some people were basically "good" and others were overtly "bad"—that is, some were sold out to the "flesh" while others exhibited what Abraham Lincoln called "the better angels of our nature." But Alexander Solzhenitsyn highlighted the impossibility of this separation when he wrote:

> *If only there were evil people somewhere insidiously committing evil deeds, and it were necessary only to separate them from the rest of us and destroy them. But the line dividing good and evil cuts through the heart of every human being. And who is willing to destroy a piece of his own heart?*[5]

The flesh seeks its own, period. The flesh enjoys personal pleasure above all things and does not give thought to the pain that many pleasures bring. It seeks to derail peace, righteousness, and legacy at all costs. And it has robbed many a man of his opportunity to lead his wife, his family, his organization, and his community.

And how does the flesh manifest itself in the lives of men? Well, consider the flesh as the root of a large tree. Then consider the potential fruit that grows on its branches as out-workings of that inner corruption of the heart:

> *Now the works of the flesh are evident: sexual immorality, impurity, sensuality, idolatry, sorcery, enmity, strife, jealousy, fits of anger, rivalries, dissentions, division, envy, drunkenness, orgies, and things like these.* (Galatians 5:19-21)

These are timeless issues with which men have struggled since the dawn of creation—but they are seemingly more alive now than ever. These works naturally occur whenever we simply let the flesh have its way in our lives. Without self-control, the flesh is in control.

Throughout the years, I've noticed four major obstacles for men on the road to self-leadership. That is to say, there are four huge road blocks that get in the way of men enjoying peace, righteousness, and legacy. Beyond that, these four obstacles also prevent men from leading others effectively. Not surprisingly, the list of works in Galatians represents all four. Every man, no matter who he is, is a potential victim.

Keep in mind that this list was compiled 2,000 years ago—that is, there's nothing new to see here. But the fact that we've never "cured" or eradicated anything on this list should catch our attention. So let's take a short but honest look at each of these in order to better understand how to avoid them on the road to self-leadership.

The first and chief obstacle is the king of all sins: P-R-I-D-E. Yes, pride is at the heart of all sins, and pride can derail any man's family, career, and pursuits. But you might say, "I don't see the word 'pride' on that list from Galatians." Yes, it's true that the word does not explicitly appear. But so many of the "works of the flesh" listed are merely subsets of the sin of pride: enmity, strife, jealousy, fits of anger, rivalries, dissentions, divisions, and envy—that's over 50 percent of the entire list!

Nothing inflates self more, magnifies self more greatly, refuses to apologize for self more often, and wishes to compare self to others more consistently. Pride prevents a man from "making things right" with his wife. Pride prevents a man from being transparent with his children and apologizing to them when he is clearly wrong. Pride causes infighting on the job or in the community or—God help us—even in churches. In short, pride keeps a man from a right relationship with God and other people. And, at the end of the day, what will God entrust to a man incapable of such relationships? Nothing of lasting value. Thus, pride makes every man unfit to lead.

Simply put, God opposes the proud. And what exactly is the definition of pride? First and foremost, pride is an attitude that refuses to honor, worship, and rely upon God. In Hosea 10:13, God chides those whose lives are filled with this sort of self-reliance: "But you have planted wickedness, you have reaped evil, you have eaten the fruit of deception. Because you have depended on your own strength [and not mine]." Yes, pride disrupts the relationship God desires to have with us. But pride also destroys the relationships that God wants us to have with others. The "pride of life" mentioned by the Apostle John (1 John 2:16) is that which causes all of us to instinctively look down on others with sneering derision. In summary, pride dismisses God, dismisses humility, dismisses humanity, and seeks only that which is best for self. And a man infected with this sort of pride is simply unfit to lead his family, his organization, and his community.

The second obstacle to self-leadership is misplaced sexual energy: "sexual immorality, impurity, sensuality . . . [and] orgies." This is arguably the most well-known obstacle only because salacious details attract more attention than any other kind. So when a man is caught up by this road block, the entire world wants to know all about it. But the issue does not originate with the action by which the man is ultimately caught. Rather, this is an issue that originates in the heart and mind. James 1:14-15 contains this stark warning: "Each man is tempted when he is lured and enticed by his own desire. Then desire when it has conceived gives birth to sin, and sin when it is fully grown brings forth death." Or, as Stephen Covey has noted, "Sow a thought, reap an action; sow an action, reap a habit; sow a habit, reap a character."[6]

If a man wants to avoid this very destructive obstacle he must begin with his thoughts. That's certainly what Jesus implied in his famous Sermon on the Mount: "You have heard it said, 'You shall not commit adultery.' But I say to you that everyone who looks at a woman with lustful intent has already committed adultery with her in his heart" (Matthew 5:27-28). Thus, the problem of misplaced sexual energy begins with how a man thinks and only then leads to how he acts.

One of the most obvious culprits that sexually corrupts a man's mind is pornography. Although some have argued that pornography has positive benefits for a man and even for his marriage, common sense, research, and years of observation vigorously argue otherwise. From the misplaced production of dopamine in the brain which results in an addiction to the sexual novelty that pornography provides to the neurological craving for that repeated novelty, pornography undermines a man's ability to cultivate true intimacy with his wife and eats away at his capacity to make and maintain a healthy commitment to one woman.

Beyond that, every man must understand the power of sexual energy and how, apart from self-control and self-leadership, it can easily derail his entire life. Just consider these words found in the book of Proverbs:

Keep your way far from [sexual immorality] ... lest you give your honor to others and your years to the merciless, lest strangers take their fill of your strength, and your labors go to the house of a foreigner, and at the end of your life you groan, when your flesh and body are consumed. (Proverbs 5:8-11)

Again, John the Apostle juxtaposed the "lust of the flesh" with his warning about "the pride of life" (1 John 2:16). These are the things that bring down men like David Haight and Jeff Sinclair. These are the things that will likewise prevent you and me from leading our families, our organizations, and our communities.

The third obstacle to self-leadership is greed. Again, though not explicitly listed in Galatians, it stands behind these works of the flesh: "idolatry . . . jealousy . . . envy." Each of these represent in their own way an unhealthy desire for something that God has not already delivered. In the ancient world, idolatry typically involved the literal worship of an image or some sort of quasi-god. In our contemporary world, idolatry usually revolves around misplaced priorities—that is, an idol is anything that displaces God as chief recipient of a man's devotion, energy, and passion. In many cases, a man's desire for more power, possessions, and position drive this idolatry. That's why the Apostle John also listed "the lust of the eyes" along with "the lust of the flesh" and the "pride of life" (1 John 2:16). In the case of jealousy and envy, a man is blinded by his desire for something that someone else has to the point that he demonstrates love for the thing he desires more than love for the person who has it. This is an attitude that runs contrary to the law of love found in the Bible—"Rejoice with those who rejoice" (Romans 12:15)—but can easily lead to actions such as thievery, embezzlement, and fraud. Whether stealing $500 or $5,000,000, a lack of self-leadership can allow greed to run wild and ruin a man relationally, professionally, and spiritually.

The fourth obstacle to self-leadership is substance addiction. The word "drunkenness" appears in Galatians, not only as a warning against the misuse of alcohol but also as a symbol for all sorts of substance addiction. In the United States, 14 million adults and 3 million teenagers (ages 13-17) abuse alcohol. Those staggering statistics represent broken families, jobs lost, careers wrecked, and lives ruined. For men, the problem is exponentially greater— some 75 percent of all abusers of alcohol are men. Not surprisingly, women are more likely to be the collateral victims of alcohol abuse in the form of abusive relationships and unwanted sexual advances or contact. Moreover, nearly 100,000 Americans die each year in alcohol related events, which makes alcohol abuse the third leading cause of preventable death in the United States. Clearly, it is very difficult for men to exercise self-leadership when they allow alcohol to take an unreasonable place in their lives. Beyond alcohol abuse, all manner of recreational and misused prescription drugs prevent millions of men from finding peace, righteousness, and legacy. Like these other obstacles grounded in the desires of the flesh, substance addiction will quickly disqualify a man for leadership.

The Keys to Self-Leadership

If the flesh is at the root of all that might prevent a man from leading himself, what is the key to self-leadership? Based on what we've already said, the answer is obvious:

Walk by the Spirit, and you will not gratify the desires of the flesh. [For] the fruit of the Spirit is . . . self control. (Galatians 5:16, 22-23)

The Spirit of God in the life of a man is the key to self-leadership. The Spirit of God is the answer to this age-old problem of the flesh. While the flesh has its by-products (we've already listed them above), the Spirit has its fruit: love, joy, peace, patience, kindness, goodness, faithfulness, gentleness, and self-control (Galatians 5:22-23). Thus, for the man who has received the Spirit of God—that is, the man who has received Jesus Christ by faith (see chapter ten for more about that)—there is at least a potential for overcoming the flesh and exercising a meaningful level of self-control. But that's easier said than done, not least because the Spirit and the flesh are locked in perpetual combat: "The desires of the flesh are against the Spirit, and the desires of the Spirit are against the flesh, for these are opposed to each other, to keep a man from doing what he ought to do" (Galatians 5:17).

As men, how do we allow the Spirit to have control? Well, there are some very practical keys for allowing the Spirit to have its way in in our lives. These are disciplines that, when followed, maximize the Spirit's foothold and minimize the grip of the flesh on our hearts and minds. But be warned: the flesh inside of you wants nothing to do with these disciplines and will try to dissuade you at all costs from embracing them and allowing them to become healthy habits. Remember, the flesh hates self-leadership. In fact, as you read about these disciplines, don't be surprised if you find yourself questioning them or coming up with quick excuses why you can't incorporate them into your life (see chapter six for a broader discussion of spiritual disciplines).

First, in order to give way to the Spirit, a man must embrace the Lordship of Jesus Christ. When someone receives Jesus Christ personally by faith, we often say that they have received Jesus as their "Savior"—that is, they have received forgiveness for their sins through Jesus' atoning sacrifice on the cross. This is a fundamental aspect of the Christian faith. But no one can truly receive Jesus as their Savior if they fail to recognize him also as their Lord. And what exactly does that mean for a man? It means that he not only freely receives the gifts of forgiveness and eternal life, but it also means that he pledges his allegiance to Jesus as the guiding principle and person of his entire life. Receiving Jesus as Savior takes but a moment; recognizing him as Lord and more completely aligning your life with his is a life-long process. Or as someone has well said, "Salvation takes a second, but Lordship takes a lifetime."

The man who acknowledges the Lordship of Jesus Christ is a man whose life is gradually but constantly changing, constantly becoming more and more obedient to the Lord Christ. This is the consistent picture of the Christian life found throughout the Bible. Jesus himself expected this sort of obedience when he asked in Luke 6:46, "Why do you call me 'Lord, Lord,' but not do what I tell you?" And Paul the Apostle described it this way in 2 Corinthians

5:15, "Jesus died for all, that those who live should no longer live for themselves for but for him who died for them and was raised again."

When a man embraces the Lordship of Jesus Christ, he is first and foremost giving his will to the Lord. And that's really the only thing we truly give to God—our will. Once we do that, everything else follows. But it is the will that must precede all other things. It's as if a man writes a check to God, signs his name, leaves the "amount" portion blank, and says, "There it is God, you fill in the amount however you like." This is a fundamental aspect of self-leadership.

As we've already discussed, the flesh absolutely HATES the Lordship of Jesus Christ. For that matter, the flesh hates the idea of submitting to anyone or anything. Yet that's exactly what must happen if a man is to lead himself, for the Lordship of Jesus Christ puts the flesh and the self in their rightful place. Or, as the old saying goes, "When self is on the cross, Christ is on the throne; but when self is on the throne, Christ is on the cross." One or the other will give way.

Second, in order to give way to the Spirit, a man must engage daily in the realm of the Spirit. This might at first sound a bit mystical, but basically it means that a man must, for lack of a better way to say it, deliberately choose to "feed the Spirit." Consider the famous Cherokee Indian legend about the two wolves:

An old Cherokee said to his grandson, "A fight is going on inside of me. It is a terrible fight between two wolves. One wolf is evil—he is anger, envy, sorrow, regret, greed, arrogance, guilt, false pride, superiority, and ego." He continued, "The other wolf is good—he is joy, peace, love, hope, humility, kindness, generosity, truth, compassion, and faith. This fight goes on inside of every person." The grandson asked, "Which wolf will win?" And the old Cherokee simply replied, "The one you feed."

Or, as Paul Harvey said in his folksy manner, "There's an election going on every day: the Lord votes for you, the devil votes against you, and you get the deciding vote."[7] Neither of these illustrations are all that far from the truth: "The one who sows to his own flesh will from the flesh reap corruption, but the one who sows to the Spirit will from the Spirit reap eternal life" (Galatians 6:8). The decision lies with the man who understands the nature of the internal battle and deliberately seeks to feed the Spirit rather than the flesh (more about feeding the Spirit in chapter six).

This is meant to be a daily discipline. Yes, attending a church or worship service once a week is great, but engaging in the realm of the Spirit only one day each week does not really help a man to "walk in the Spirit"—the flesh is simply too entrenched. But when a man engages in the realm of the Spirit daily and at numerous points throughout each day, he effectively "sows to the Sprit." This is where personal and private time in the Bible and in prayer make a big difference in the life of a more elite man. This is where listening to some type of Christian worship music while driving in the car makes a big difference. This is where reading a book related to the Christian life or a biography describing the life of a great Christian makes a difference. Indeed, the man who consistently engages the realm of the Spirit will find himself better equipped to lead himself and to lead others.

Third, in order to give way to the Spirit, a man must receive the Truth regularly. This happens when a man privately reads his Bible, yes. But I have for some time argued that every man needs three voices of Biblical Truth in his life. These voices are those of Bible teachers and other men who faithfully and without apology teach and speak the Word of God. The first voice must be the man's pastor. Every man who would lead himself should be under the regular teaching of a man of God who doesn't shrink from telling him the Truth about God, about life, about the condition of his own heart, and about the hope that Jesus provides for realizing peace, righteousness, and legacy. A man should choose for his pastor a man who is not afraid to deliver "hard teaching"—not so much in terms of delivery (shouting or pounding a fist on the pulpit, per se) but in terms of content. He should choose for his pastor a man whom the Spirit uses to place the bony finger of conviction on any number of issues and press down with enough force to inspire change.

But the pastor's voice is not enough. For most men, they won't hear from their pastor more than once each week, and that is not enough Truth for a man to grow beyond the basics. That's why I say every man needs three voices—one should be his pastor while the other two can be any other teachers of the Bible who, like the pastor, sincerely challenge the man to be better, think better, and do better. These other voices might belong to a trusted friend in the local area or even a selected teacher whose messages are broadcast on the radio or internet or who teaches a small-group Bible study the man attends. Either way, a more elite man will deliberately seek voices of Biblical Truth that he can hear on a regular basis.

Fourth, in order to give way to the Spirit you must meet with other men to discuss faith and the things of the Spirit. This could be in the setting of a formal Bible study or prayer group. This could be a group who gathers to play basketball and pray. This could be a group that eats breakfast and talks about their faith. Regardless of the specific context, the group must be relatively small—no more than four or five men. There is a lot of goodness in men getting together to encourage one another and talk about what God is doing in their lives. The small size of the group will facilitate a greater degree of transparency. And as men become more transparent, they begin to get real with each other and truly encourage each other. At the same time, these men must open themselves up to accountability—that is, they must allow other men in the group to provide spiritual and emotional oversight and ask the hard questions about the man's private life. As with anything else that potentially brings a man closer to God, the flesh despises external accountability, which is precisely why a man must seek a small and transparent context of accountability.

The Marks of Self-Leadership

There are certain marks that accompany self-leadership. In other words, when a man is truly engaging in and winning the battel with the flesh, there are certain things that will be true of him and his life. First, a man who is leading himself will reject entitlement. Second, a man who is leading himself will embrace accountability. Third, a man who is leading himself will cast off hypocrisy. And last, a man who is leading himself will cultivate trust. Let's talk about each.

Self-Leadership Rejects Entitlement

Do you remember when Tiger Woods got his hand caught in the proverbial cookie jar—make that *several* cookie jars? He had it all: a superlative professional golf career that eclipsed all records, an incredible amount of wealth, immense celebrity status, a beautiful wife, and millions of adoring fans. Yet, in spite of all of that, he wanted more. But then it all came crashing down, and to this day he's never really recovered professionally or relationally. Do you remember the short press conference he held a few months after revelations came out regarding his many extramarital sexual relationships? He didn't say much, but what he said was very telling: "I convinced myself that normal rules didn't apply. I felt that I had worked hard my entire life and deserved to enjoy all the temptations around me. I felt I was entitled."[8]

In a world that seemingly caters to us and urges us to enjoy any and all pleasures and, at least in our own minds, revolves around us, it's easy to get a sense of entitlement, isn't it? *I need this. I deserve this. No one will deny me this.* No matter your social status, no matter your economic status, and no matter your spiritual status, the siren song of self-interest and entitlement gently call us to abandon self-control and restraint in favor of indulgence and momentary pleasure. Sadly, a man can lose sight of the high calling of duty to others and duty to something bigger than himself. In short, entitlement kills a sense of external duty.

A perfect example of entitlement gone wild is found in the story of David, the King of Israel:

> *In the spring of the year, the time when kings go out to battle, David sent Joab and his army to attack the Ammonites. But David remained at Jerusalem.* (2 Samuel 11:1)

Those familiar with the Bible instantly recognize these words as the introduction to one of the most sordid tales of entitlement that led to gross sexual sin and murder. As the story goes, David remained in the rear instead of going forward to war with his men. As he lounged around the palace, he noticed a beautiful woman named Bathsheba (whose husband was a soldier fighting in the war), sent for her, and had a sexual encounter with her. When she discovered that she was pregnant with David's child and told him so, he deliberately had her husband killed in battle to cover his tracks. Ultimately, however, God sent a prophet to confront David about his transgression, and David begged for God's forgiveness.

David had a God-given duty to his men and to the kingdom, and yet he lost sight of that in favor of something he knew was morally off-limits. Yes, he had many accomplishments under his belt, but like Jeff Sinclair, he "squandered a fortune of life's blessings." He somehow convinced himself that staying back in Jerusalem while his men fought on the front lines was acceptable. And when he gazed upon Bathsheba, he might as well have uttered Tiger's words of regret: "I convinced myself that normal rules didn't apply. I felt that I had worked hard my entire life and deserved to enjoy all the temptations around me. I felt I was entitled."

That famous story about David inspired, among other things, a widely-read 1993 article entitled "The Bathsheba Syndrome: The Ethical Failure of Successful Leaders."[9] Written by Dean C. Ludwig and Clinton O. Longenecker, the article argues that leaders who experience success are often poorly equipped to deal with privilege, pressure, and unrestrained control. In David's case, he took advantage of his position to gain what he wanted. He had won many battles in his lifetime. Surely he was entitled to stay home and take care of himself, right? The sad thing is that, as the article suggests, he likely deceived himself through complacency and loss of focus. The result was that he was taken completely unaware by his sense of entitlement and lack of self-leadership. He was the first among many leaders to give way to the Bathsheba Syndrome.

As men, we must be aware that all of this—and much, much more—could happen to any one of us. Do you have a happy marriage? It could be blasted to bits by a moment clouded by entitlement and selfish decision-making. Do you enjoy a position of professional leadership and influence? You could lose it all in a skinny minute if you're not leading yourself first. Don't think it couldn't happen to you!

Self-Leadership Embraces Accountability

A senior Army leader once told me, "Leaders, by nature, hate accountability." That's a strong statement, but it carries a lot of truth. After all, leaders, especially strong leaders, want a free hand to develop and pursue their vision for an organization. They want to accomplish a mission according to their own understanding of what must happen and for what reason. "Why waste time reporting to higher? If they would mind their own business and stay out of mine, I'd really be able to make things happen around here!"

But strong leaders aren't the only ones who resist accountability. Just about everyone finds answering to someone else distasteful. No man likes to have his feet held to the metaphorical fire. But, because of self-deception, few men can objectively look at themselves and assess weaknesses and pending disaster. And that's why being accountable and embracing accountability is a fundamental discipline of self-leadership.

General Creighton Abrams said many years ago, "Never hesitate to look in the dark corners of your organization."[10] Isn't that exactly what most of us would rather NOT do personally? It's easy to leave well enough alone. After all, if we did peek into those dusty corners of our lives, we might discover something that needs to change. That's why it's important to invite someone we know and trust to ask us the hard questions and peek into our dark corners. Some time ago, I heard Major General Doug Carver, who at the time was the Army's Chief of Chaplains, tell of a time when a senior Army leader came and handed him a single key on a string. Chaplain Carver said, "What's this all about?" The man replied, "This is the key to my life. I want you to have total and complete access to my life—you can ask any question about any part of my life, examine any part of my life, and dig into the deepest, darkest corner. I need you to hold me accountable."

I know what some of you guys are thinking. You're thinking, "All of that seems a little excessive, don't you think?" But questioning the necessity of that sort of accountability is exactly why millions of men are blade-running in their private lives, living right on the edge of making foolish decisions in secret that, without a course correction, will spell personal and professional disaster.

As a man, be mindful that you must embrace external accountability. You simply do not have the ability to police yourself absolutely. Self-leadership embraces accountability because self-leadership understands what's at stake.

Major Phil Kramer

Self-Leadership Reduces Hypocrisy

Every leader knows that the quickest way to lose the confidence of his followers is to engage in blatant hypocrisy. Telling the team to do one thing and then personally going in a different direction will kill any leader's influence. Likewise, forbidding a certain decision or action only to decide or act in that forbidden manner will deplete a leader's bank account with his subordinates. In short, hypocrisy is the number-one roadblock to leadership success.

If that is true, then why do so many leaders engage in hypocrisy? In a nutshell, it's because they care more about themselves than they care about anyone else. The allure of hypocrisy is real because, at the end of the day, many people want to serve themselves and please themselves. And those in leadership positions are most susceptible because they often have access to privileges and amenities that subordinates don't have. And when they take advantage of that access, their subordinates note well and remember.

The classic example revolves around food at Ranger School. Keep in mind that most Ranger students are on the verge of starvation at any given time in the 62-day course, so in many cases food is almost more valuable than gold. (In fact, I can remember a few times when students bought another student's MRE—his pre-packaged and tasteless "meal ready to eat"—for upwards of $50!) And when it's time to eat, all eyes are on the food and the person distributing it. In most cases, the students will eat an MRE, a "meal ready to eat." These pre-packaged, mostly-dehydrated meals come in brown plastic bags marked on the outside with black lettering describing the meal contained inside. Each MRE box contains 12 uniquely-different meals. So when a Ranger student in a leadership position—maybe squad leader or platoon sergeant—brings a box of MREs into the patrol base, it's like Pavlov ringing the bell that causes the dogs to salivate. Once that box is opened, the students are supposed to file by and simply grab an MRE from the box—no looking, no rifling through to box to find a favorite meal, just "grab it and go." But what if the leader who brought in the box knows that there's a certain meal in the box he really wants? What if he digs through the meals and grabs that one meal before the rest of the students can file by? Well, that might not seem like such a terrible thing outside the confines of Ranger School, but selectively picking an MRE for yourself rather than blindly grabbing one and moving out is a serious offense—not to mention that the leader should eat last, not first. What will the students do if they see this kind of selfish behavior? Most likely they will ensure that the transgressor does not complete Ranger School. He will at least be a marked man for the rest of the course.

There's no place like Ranger School to show a young man just how weak he can become when placed in a situation with little food, little sleep, and mountains of stress. Even the slightest comfort goes a long way to build personal morale, so it's always tempting while in a leadership position to help oneself to something extra. But self-leadership prevents one from doing that very thing. It doesn't look to comfort itself primarily. If anything, the true leader will look for ways to take care of his men before he takes care of himself.

The man who understands the concept of self-leadership knows two specific truths. He knows that: (1) he is no better than anyone else and (2) he must set the example for others to follow. Self-leadership begins and ends with those two thoughts. And the result is that a more elite man is never thinking about how he can care only for himself—he eagerly wants to know how he can care for others consistently and meaningfully.

Self-Leadership Cultivates Trust

If there's one thing that every leader needs, its trust. This is true in every imaginable realm where a man might lead. As a husband, as a father, as a leader in the professional world, community, and church—you name it. Without trust, a man simply cannot lead.

Specifically, every leader needs a three-dimensional trust. First, he needs the trust of those he leads—do they know they can count on him to lead them consistently in the right direction? Do they know that he's looking out for their best interests? Next, he needs the trust of those who hold him accountable. Do they have confidence in his leadership? Does he need constant supervision, or can he excel with minimal guidance and oversight? Simply put, can he get the job done? And last, he needs to be able to trust those he leads.

Consistent self-leadership answers the mail on all three of these dimensions. When a man consistently proves that he is worthy of trust through avoiding the pitfalls that excessive self-indulgence creates, people will follow him. When he has demonstrated consistency in sound judgment and cultivation of leadership vision, people will follow him. When, through taking charge of himself, he models integrity on a daily basis, people will follow him. We could even say that a deliberate agenda of self-improvement and development as a leader is part of self-leadership—and people follow competent leaders. Likewise, a man willing to take charge of himself and exercise self-control also enjoys the trust and confidence of those who hold him accountable. Conversely, those who cannot lead themselves are a pain to those who supervise them: "As vinegar to the teeth and smoke to the eyes, so is the sluggard to those who send him" (Proverbs 10:26). To be sure, a man of discipline who can lead himself will never lack for employment or opportunity. And through his example, he will equip those who follow him to have the same discipline and self-control.

Self Leadership: If the Gold Should Rust

There's a lot riding on a man's ability to take charge of himself, to exercise self-control, and to live a disciplined life. His position as leader is at stake—be it husband, father, professional leader, or leader in his community and church. We began this chapter with three examples of men who failed to lead themselves and in the process lost their opportunity to lead others. Beyond that, we could mention the tens of thousands of men who, each year, lose their position of family leadership through a failure to lead themselves to do the right things morally and personally.

But let's also think for a moment about those who are led. What happens to them when their leaders fail? Are they part of the collateral damage? I am reminded of an ancient story entitled "The Canterbury Tales" written by Geoffrey Chaucer around the year 1400. The story centers upon a group of some two dozen pilgrims of various social classes and positions who are traveling to the town of Canterbury. One of the pilgrims is a lowly parson, a minister in charge of a small flock of parishioners. While Chaucer paints many of the pilgrims in cynical and critical terms, he casts this simple pastor in the best light possible. He was "poor, but rich in holy thought and work" and diligently visited his people "in either rain or thunder" regardless of whether he himself was "sick or vexed." But the high point of Chaucer's description comes when he described the parson's consistency:

This fine example to his sheep he gave:
He always did good works before he taught them.
His words were from the gospel as he caught them,
And this good saying he would add thereto:
"If the gold should rust, what shall the iron do?"
For if a priest be foul in whom we trust,
No wonder that the ignorant goes to rust.
And it's a shame (as every priest should keep
In mind), a dirty shepherd and clean sheep.
For every priest should an example give,
By his own cleanness, how his sheep should live.[11]

The classic line here should serve as warning to leaders everywhere to seriously consider their responsibility to lead by example—to lead themselves first: "If the gold should rust, what shall the iron do?" Truth be told, many leaders who fail often take some of their followers with them. That is, through their lack of leadership and poor example, others learn how to neglect to lead themselves, too.

The good news is that self-control, discipline, and self-leadership are not outside the realm of possibilities for any man. Indeed, every man who seeks to understand the internal battle between the flesh and the Spirit can, at the end of the day, take charge of himself and choose to do the right thing. Only such men are qualified to lead others in the way of peace, righteousness, and legacy.

3
Team Leadership: A Man's Highest Calling

The U.S. Army Ranger School is often billed as "the Army's toughest course and premier small unit tactics and leadership school." The Ranger Handbook, the "Bible" for all Ranger students, frontloads the topic of leadership in chapter one and describes leadership as "the most essential element of combat power." Few Army schools place a greater leadership demand upon junior soldiers than Ranger School. And every Ranger knows that he must be prepared at all times to lead, either through appointment of position or by circumstance whereby he must hastily replace a fallen or fired leader. Team leadership is every Ranger's life blood.

Just as every Ranger must be ready to lead a team, so every man must understand his God-given calling and responsibility to lead his family, his organization, and his community. As we saw in the last chapter, self-leadership is vital for any man who wants to impact and influence his family, his organization, and the world around him. If nothing else, it qualifies a man to stand before others with a clear conscience and say simply yet profoundly, "Follow me!" But self-leadership is only a means to a greater end. For every man, team leadership is the ultimate goal.

God has called every man first and foremost to lead himself. Beyond that, God gives every man certain spheres of influence and leadership. Husbands are called to lead their wives. Fathers are called to lead their children. Men of all professional stripes are called to lead in whatever capacity they find themselves. Men are also called to lead in their communities. To be a man is to be called to lead.

Every man who leads must grasp the fundamentals of leadership. Those fundaments are not mysterious or hidden—rather, they are open secrets that every man can discover and implement. In fact, I've often said that the basics of leadership are like the menu in a Mexican restaurant. Think about it: Mexican food only has about four to five key ingredients—things like meat, cheese, rice, beans, and a few vegetables. And yet, even though there are only a few key ingredients, the menus at Mexican restaurants are often crowded with well over 100 meals to order, all made up of roughly the same few ingredients. And so it is with leaders and leadership principles. There may be 100 different leaders in a large organization and each has his personal leadership philosophy. But the same leadership fundamentals emerge over and over again across the 100 leaders.

Team leadership is a man's highest calling, and this chapter highlights several fundamentals of team leadership as found in the story of Nehemiah, a man who had both a tremendous faith in God and also almost-unlimited leadership capacity, ability, and energy. Nehemiah was a Hebrew leader who, among many others, was living in a foreign land hundreds of miles to the east of Jerusalem. He was employed by the king of Persia as an advisor and key servant. Day after day, he longed for his homeland and for Jerusalem, the Holy City. Then one day, some people came to see him who had recently been in Jerusalem. He no doubt said, "Tell me about Jerusalem— bless me with a report that I may dream of its wonders." But what they shared with him was nothing short of a nightmare. They reported that the city was in ruins, the walls were shattered, and the gates burned with fire. That report hit Nehemiah like a thunderclap, and he did the only thing he could do—he went to God in deep, sustained, and soul-revealing prayer. And God led him to believe that he should return to Jerusalem to spearhead the rebuilding of the walls around the city.

And then he began to lead.

He returned to Jerusalem with workers, materials, and other resources. He conducted a personal assessment of the damage to the wall. He gathered the people together, cast his vision, and galvanized their hearts and minds. Along the way, he dealt with internal conflict and external friction. Throughout the entire project, he trusted God and walked by faith. And at the end of it all, he accomplished his leadership objective. It's really an amazing leadership story. And not surprisingly, numerous authors of books on leadership have used Nehemiah as the backdrop—books like *Hand Me Another Brick: Timeless Lessons on Leadership* by Chuck Swindoll and *The Nehemiah Factor* by Frank Page, just to name a few.[1]

Team Leadership and The Center of Gravity

As a team leader, Nehemiah demonstrated the tremendous power that leadership energy can provide an organization and an effort. Nehemiah was what I call a "catalyst" leader—that is, God used him as a single point of gravity to accomplish something spiritually and eternally significant. (It's important to note that another man named Ezra also played a singular role in the rebuilding of Jerusalem, but the wall was Nehemiah's "baby" and he was the catalyst leader who led its rebuilding.)

Those familiar with the book of Nehemiah might say, "But the secret to the rebuilding of the wall was that 'the people had a mind to work'" (Nehemiah 4:6). That may be true to some degree, but consider that those same people were not working before Nehemiah showed up—rather, they were content to sit around and feel sorry for themselves. They had great potential, but they did not have a catalyst leader. As any good leader does, Nehemiah highlighted the people's efforts in Nehemiah 4:6 instead of his own contributions when he told the story of the rebuilding of the walls. But make no mistake about it: Nehemiah was the catalyst; he was the center of gravity. And he demonstrated the power of a strong leader. Or as Alexander the Great reportedly said, "I would rather have an army of sheep led by a lion than an army of lions led by a sheep."

Of course, when Nehemiah assumed the position of catalyst leader, he also assumed what I call the "blessed burden of leadership responsibility." After all, everyone wants to see the results of catalyst leadership, but not everyone is willing to experience the conflict and friction that often confront a man who exerts leadership energy. As we will see below, Nehemiah certainly faced his share of opposition and friction. But he stayed committed to the task at hand. He maintained his position as the catalyst leader.

And so can you.

Insight

Every leadership endeavor begins with insight. As we see in Nehemiah's narrative, he arrived on the scene in Jerusalem and conducted an honest assessment of the situation. Times were indeed hard, but rather than being discouraged by what he saw, he was driven by it:

I went to Jerusalem and was there three days. . . . Then I went out by night by the Valley Gate to the Dragon Spring and to the Dung Gate, and I inspected the walls of Jerusalem that were broken down and its gates that had been destroyed by fire. Then I went on to the Fountain Gate and to the King's Pool. Then I went up in the night by the valley and inspected the wall, and

I turned back and entered the Valley Gate, and so returned.
(Nehemiah 2:11-15)

The first thing we must understand is that every leader worth his salt has the ability to see *and foresee*. Wayne Gretsky, the hall-of-fame hockey star, once said, "I'm not the biggest or the fastest. But when I skate, I don't skate to where the puck is, I skate to where the puck will be." That's called the ability to foresee. Or think about the entertainment genius Walt Disney. At the opening of Disney World in Orlando in 1972, someone said to Lillian Disney, Walt's widow, "This is so magnificent, It's too bad that Walt isn't here to see it" (he passed away a few years earlier). But Lillian Disney replied, "Oh, but he did see it. That's why it's here—because he saw it before it ever came into being."[3] That's an amazing statement since only a decade earlier, the site had been nothing more than a central Florida swamp. But Disney saw something there that others could not see.

As he conducted his assessment by night, what do you think Nehemiah saw? Yes, of course, he saw the walls broken down, the burned gates, and the rubble and debris. But is that all that he saw? I would argue that he saw much more than that. His leadership insight allowed him to see beyond what was to what could be. And that's a key leadership fundamental.

John Maxwell, the great leadership guru, has often pointed out the difference between a leader and manager. According to Maxwell, a manager may be very gifted at maintaining direction and momentum, but he's not necessarily equipped to successfully change either for the better. A leader, on the other hand, has the ability to change both direction and momentum toward even more positive results.[4] Nehemiah was not sent by God to manage the rubble and debris—he was sent to lead the people beyond their limited scope of reality to an entirely new reality.

Someone has said that you can gauge a leader based on the size of the problems he tackles. If that is true, then Nehemiah was a king-sized leader. And when he shared his insight and vision with the people, they knew immediately that they were not dealing with a keeper of the status quo or merely a manager who would help them to maintain their current direction and momentum (or lack thereof). Rather, they knew they were dealing with a change agent with big plans:

> *Then I said to them, "You see the trouble we are in, how Jerusalem lies in ruins with its gates burned. Come, let us build the wall of Jerusalem, that we may no longer suffer derision" And I told them of the hand of my God that had been good upon me, and also of the words the king had spoken to me. And they said, "Let us arise and build." So they strengthened their hands for the good work.* (Nehemiah 2:17-18)

Nehemiah's insight set the stage for great days to come. He came prepared to lead and he would not rest until he had accomplished his task. He demonstrated a tremendous amount of leadership energy and, through is leadership, he galvanized the people's will toward the task at hand.

Courage

Leaders who have great insight also need great courage, for anytime someone with insight rises up and says, "Follow me," someone else is bound to say, "Sit down and shut up! We're not interested in change." That's exactly what happened in Nehemiah's day. He knew that there would be opposition, but he drove on with what God had called him to do. And it wasn't long after he shared his vision and put the people to work that opposition mounted:

When Sanballat and Tobiah and the Arabs and the Ammonites and the Ashdodites heard that the repairing of the walls of Jerusalem was going forward and that the breaches were beginning to be closes, they were very angry. And they all plotted together to come and fight against Jerusalem and to cause confusion in it. And we prayed to our God and set a guard as a protection against them day and night (Nehemiah 4:7-8)

Nehemiah knew that opposition would come, and he could have chosen to stay in Persia and enjoy his position and comfort. But God had placed a bigger desire on his heart and he followed it—he took a tremendous risk. But as Andy Stanley has often said, "For every true leader, there will come a time when his desire for progress will overcome his reluctance to take a risk." Yes, Nehemiah shared the outlook of Ronald Reagan who, responding to the explosion of the space shuttle *Challenger* in 1986, said, "The future does not belong to the fainthearted. The future belongs to the brave."

I believe that Nehemiah's courage was rooted in his faith. As you scan the book of Nehemiah, you see in nearly every chapter a prayer that he prayed. Most often, he's praying in the midst of conflict and opposition. When opposition came—and it came quite often—he didn't waste a lot of time dealing with it. Rather, he prayed and moved on. Michael Catt has said, "When problems arise you can consider them, but don't take them into consideration." In many ways, Nehemiah considered his problems and then just turned them over to God. That's not to say he didn't take action to address the problems (see below for more on that). But he didn't dwell on the opposition; he dwelt on what God had called him to do. I like what Adrian Rogers said about Nehemiah and his habit of telling God about his enemies and asking him to deal with them rather than trying to wrestle endlessly with his enemies: "A bulldog can whip a skunk, but it's not worth it."

Character

I've studied the book of Nehemiah for almost 25 years. When I first read through the book, I was instantly impressed by what Nehemiah did and what he accomplished. But as the years have gone by and I've repeatedly read the book through the eyes of experience and age, I've become more impressed by who Nehemiah was than what Nehemiah accomplished. I've become convinced that Nehemiah was a man of tremendous, consistent, and authentic spiritual character.

Andy Stanley has said, "People buy into the leader before they buy into the leadership."[5] I believe Nehemiah gave the people good reason to buy into who he was before they bought into his vision and plan. In plain language, he was the "real deal"—a man whose character was evident to all. And that made him a very compelling figure for those he led.

Nehemiah was a man of consistent prayer and spiritual practice. As mentioned above, you can't go too many verses into the book of Nehemiah without seeing him go to God in prayer. Long before he developed a plan, he prayed. As he implemented his plan, he prayed. When opposition arose, he prayed. As the task was nearing completion, he prayed. And even after the task was accomplished, he prayed.

It's important to note that Nehemiah was what we might call a layman—that is, he was not a priest, religious leader, or minister. In other words, he was not a "professional" believer in God. He was, rather, simply a man appointed to lead who knew deep down inside that he needed God to be part of his calculus as a leader. He was very gifted—yes, exceptionally gifted—but he wisely did not depend on himself and his abilities. Instead, he ultimately trusted in God. In other words, he avoided eating what God calls "the bread of deception" as mentioned in Hosea 10:13 – "You have eaten the bread of deception because you have relied upon your own abilities and not upon me."

Someone once told me, "Phil, never lower your bucket into your own well; be sure to lower your bucket into God's well." Essentially, that's a metaphor for depending upon God and relying upon him rather than depending upon yourself. That's a great word for leaders, especially. The private character of a leader will ultimately determine his success in public. Or, as Michael Catt has said, "An organization never rises above the level of its leadership. A leader never rises above the level of his prayer life. The level of your prayer life is determined by your character."[6] If that is true, then it's safe to say that Nehemiah was a man of character and prayer.

But in addition to being a man of consistent prayer and spiritual practice, Nehemiah was also a man of servant leadership. In other words, he demonstrated in tangible ways that he wasn't doing his job for self-promotion or to feather his own nest. In fact, he demonstrated just the opposite:

From the time that I was appointed to be their governor in the land of Judah, from the twentieth year to the thirty-second year of Artaxerxes the king, twelve years, neither I nor my brothers ate the food allowance of the governor. The former governors who were before me laid heavy burdens on the people and took from them for their daily ration forty shekels of silver. Even their servants lorded it over the people. But I did not do so, because of the fear of God. I also persevered in the work on this wall, and we acquired no land, and all my servants were gathered there for the work. Moreover, there were at my table 150 men, Jews and officials, besides those who came to us from the nations that were around us. Now what was prepared at my expense for each day was one ox and six choice sheep and birds, and every ten days all kinds of wine in abundance. Yet for all this I did not

demand the food allowance of the governor, because the service
was too heavy on this people. (Nehemiah 5:14-18)

Nehemiah was a leader who cared deeply for his constituents and
did not simply see them as nameless human resources who merely
served as fodder for his grand scheme. Evidently, his predecessors did
not have that same compassion. They as well as their servants took
advantage of their positions, but Nehemiah would have not of that,
because "the service was too heavy on the people."

Nehemiah could have assumed the role of a "celebrity" leader. You
know what I mean when I say a "celebrity" leader? Celebrity leaders are
very obvious in who they are—after all, they seek the spotlight and make
everything about themselves. They must constantly maintain a place in
the spotlight and they become especially annoyed when someone else
gets the attention they think they rightfully deserve. But few celebrity
leaders are people of real character. In fact, when the truth is known,
their private lives typically look much different than their pubic personas.

And by the way, I also believe that Nehemiah's ability to build
consensus among the people hinged on his character. He cultivated
buy-in across a broad audience, and he did so primarily because
the people recognized that he was the "real deal." He wasn't in this
endeavor primarily for himself, and the people saw that.

Action

Nehemiah was a man of character and prayer. But he was also a
man of action. He had a deep and abiding faith in God, but he was
also a man able to move the enterprise down the field and toward the
end zone. That's what makes Nehemiah so endearing as a leader: he
had the perfect balance between faith and action.

I'm certain that a few cynical bystanders heard Nehemiah pitch
his vision to the people back in chapter two. One scoffer might have

though, "This guy talks a good game. But as every mother knows, it's a lot easier to conceive than to deliver!" Or maybe, if a Texan had been in the crowd, he might have heard, "This guy is all hat and no cattle." But Nehemiah was much more than just talk. As a leader, he knew that he needed to deliver, and that's exactly what he did. He reminds me of a little poem I heard some time ago:

> *A tiger met a lion as they sat beside the pool,*
> *Said the tiger to the lion, "Why are you roaring like a fool?"*
> *"That's not foolish," said the lion with a twinkle in his eye,*
> *"They call me the king of the beasts because I advertise!"*
> *A rabbit heard them talking and ran home like a streak,*
> *He thought he'd try the lion's plan, but he only made a squeak.*
> *A fox came to investigate and had his lunch in woods.*
> *And so my friends when you advertise, be sure you've got the goods!*[7]

Nehemiah had "the goods." He was a decision maker who recognized that leaders must lead. Yes, he was a consensus builder, but he also demonstrated that the ability to build a consensus does not equate to an inability to make an executive decision. He considered all the fact, he consulted with his leadership . . . and then he made a decision and got to work. He planned, and then he execute the plan. That reminds of Coach John McKay, who led the Tampa Bay Buccaneer football team when they were so abysmal back in the 1970s and early 1980s. After one especially terrible game, a reporter said, "Coach, what did you think of your team's execution out there today?" McKay shot back, "My team's execution? I'm all in favor of it!"[8]

The context of Nehemiah's decisive nature was his overall leadership energy. While he rested appropriately, he was not a man of leisure. He always had his hands on the plough and maintained contact with his people and projects. I like how Pastor Brian Jones puts it: "For leaders, there's no substitute for hustle."[9] Or, as Pastor

Ronnie Floyd has noted, "Nobody who starts his day at eight o'clock builds anything great for God. The average guy begins his day at eight o'clock, and average does not build greatness."[10]

When I think about leaders of action, I think about my father-in-law and his brother. Their family has been in the cattle business down in Florida since the Civil War—my wife's a sixth-generation Floridian. Forty-five years ago, my father-in-law and his brother had a few thousand acres and a mountain of debt when their dad passed away with no estate planning. But they dug their heels in a worked hard. They took action. Now they've got a ton of land and a ton of cows. When I first married into that family, I thought I was going to sit on the front porch in the morning, sipping on a mint julep and watching the field hands go out to work. Well, I quickly discovered that I was one of the field hands! Nobody sits idle on that ranch.

Nehemiah was a man of devoted action. He saw his vocation as a calling from God and poured himself into it. He wasn't one of these guys who saw his job simply as a means to finance his weekend hobbies. He had leadership energy and consistently applied it to the task at hand through God's strength and for God's glory.

But in the midst of that decisive action, Nehemiah also displayed a certain leadership finesse. You never see him pulling a "bull-in-a-china-shop" leadership moment. Yes, there were times when he was angry with others and with the circumstances, but he never let it affect his leadership wisdom. Nehemiah understood that, given a reasonable amount of leadership and encouragement, most people would eventually come on board. Real leadership doesn't have to unreasonable force anything.

This reminds me about one of the first times I ever worked cows with my wife's family. My father-in-law and I went to one of their ranches on four-wheelers to gather cows for cow work the next day. We went back to one palmetto patch and saw two cows off by themselves. We opened a gap in the fence and then he said we needed to get the cows to go through the gap. Well, I went blasting away into those palmettos on my four-wheeler, determined to get those cows to do exactly what I wanted. For probably fifteen minutes, I went this way but the cows went that way. Then when I went that way, the cows went this way. All the while, I was blasting away with that four-wheeler and making a lot of noise but not making any headway with the cows. No matter how hard I tried, I could NOT get those cows to concentrate on that gap. When I finally gave up, my father-in-law slowly drove his four-wheeler over my way and gingerly moved toward those cows, and they quietly walked through that gap. I'm sure he thought I was the biggest knuckle-head in the world! But I learned something that day about leading cows and took away a great application for leading people, too.

A Simple Commitment to Leadership

If you are a man, then God has called you to lead. He has called you to lead your family. He has called you to lead in your church. He has called you to lead in your organization and in your community. But what exactly does that look like? And how do we apply the principles of insight, courage, character, and action to our own leadership endeavors? Let me give just a few examples.

First, determine to set the spiritual pace for your family. Ask God to give you insight into what your family could become through your spiritual leadership. Is your wife a better Christian and more like Jesus Christ because of your leadership and influence in her life? Is she truly challenged to love God and love people more because of you? Or is she the spiritual pace-setter in your home and you're just along for the ride? Think about this challenge found in the book of Ephesians:

Husbands, love your wives as Christ loved the church and gave himself up for her, that he might sanctify her, having cleansed her by the washing of water with the word, so that he might present the church to himself in splendor, without spot or wrinkle or any such thing, that she might be holy without blemish. (Ephesians 5:25-27)

Sometimes this takes courage, especially if you've been a spiritually-passive man in your home. Maybe your family doesn't even go to church, or goes only on special occasions. If you decide to take the spiritual lead, your family might not enthusiastically embrace your leadership at first. But don't give up—take action and lead.

Another way you can lead your family is to lead your children (and grandchildren, if you have them) to a saving knowledge of Jesus Christ and equip them in their faith. Studies have shown that as many as 70 percent of "church kids" abandon their faith and church attendance when they leave home. And of that 70 percent, only half ever return. Why? Most experts agree: they never truly had a saving knowledge of Jesus Christ—that is, they were never really converted.

Unfortunately, most "church" parents are content if their kids "make a decision" for Jesus when they're young, attend church on a regular basis in their teenage years, and stay out of any significant trouble. But while these kids are entertained with programs at church, they're never been challenged to be sure and certain of their own salvation in the face of questions and doubts. Yes, take your children to church consistently. But ensure that whatever they receive from a pastor or youth pastor is just gravy compared to the meat-and-potatoes leadership and equipping they're getting from you in your home. That requires character and action from you as a dad. And once your child or grandchild makes a commitment to Jesus Christ, watch them over time. If you're not seeing any real fruit in their lives, ask them about it and challenge them to live according to their commitment. Again, this requires courage and leadership energy.

Second, you should be a leader in your church. How can you do that, especially if you're not a pastor or senior layman? You can lead by mentoring younger men to become leaders in your church. One of the biggest challenges churches face today is a lack of quality, mature, self-starting leaders. Your responsibility as a man is first to be that kind of leader and then to deliberately, energetically, and strategically mentor other young men to follow your example. As a man, can you name one or two young men who are "under your wing" as a leader? Sometimes, sadly, we become too caught up in ourselves to see the value of this type of leader development. But I like Michael Catt's warning for church leaders over the age of fifty: (1) don't resent the next generation, (2) don't hold on to power too long, (3) don't get cynical because they don't do it like you do it, and (4) rejoice in what God is doing in the next generation.[11]

Another way that you can and should lead in your church is to appoint yourself president of your pastor's fan club. Let's face it: full-time ministry can be a tough and lonely existence. Am I overstating my case when I say that most pastors are over-worked, under-paid, and under-appreciated? When was the last time you sent your pastor of hand-written note telling him how much his ministry means to you? Or how about the last time you took him out to eat and talked about something other than *your* problems? Or when was the last time you texted him during the week and mentioned something specific from his sermon—just to let him know that you were listening? As president of your pastor's fan club, you should do these things and lead other men to do the same. Even a small word of encouragement could go much farther than you realize.

Men Lead the Way

Leading is a calling, a privilege, and an opportunity. Nehemiah clearly heard God's call on his life to return to Jerusalem with insight, courage, character, and action. I pray that you likewise hear God's call to lead your family, your church, your organization, and your community. Leadership is God's highest calling on your life.

4

I Will Always Endeavor: Fear God and Take Your Own Part

African big-game hunter. Medal of Honor recipient. Amazon River explorer. Founder of the Boone and Crockett Club. Cattle rancher. Oh, and did I mention President of the United States?

Such were the many lives of Theodore Roosevelt, who, though born with asthma and other childhood ailments, willed his way into the pantheon of our nation's greatest men. Ardently advocating a "strenuous life" of physical vigor, courageous daring, and a relentless pursuit of big dreams, Roosevelt was a man's man in every way.

And did he ever have a way with words.

Whole volumes of his speeches and quotes have been published and praised, but perhaps the most celebrated is found in his "Man in the Arena" speech:

It is not the critic who counts; not the man who points out how the strong man stumbles, or where the doer of deeds could have done them better. The credit belongs to the man who is actually in the arena, whose face is marred by dust and sweat and blood; who strives valiantly; who does actually strive to do the deeds; who knows the great enthusiasms, the great devotions; who spends

himself in a worthy cause; who at best knows in the end the triumph
of high achievement, and who at the worst, if he fails, at least fails
while daring greatly, so that his place shall never be with those cold
and timid souls who neither know victory nor defeat.[1]

Although flowery and melodramatic by today's standards, this
was everyday language for Roosevelt. After all, he seriously saw
himself as the perpetual man in the arena. Indeed, for him, every
day was a cause for which to strive valiantly. Every day was marred,
at least metaphorically, by dust, sweat, and blood, and—more often
than not— every day ended with the triumph of high achievement.

I've always been intrigued by a particular trait of this man in
Roosevelt's arena—namely, that he knows "the great enthusiasms."
Roosevelt doesn't elaborate on exactly what these great enthusiasms
are, but they sound pretty impressive. And, judging by a review
of Roosevelt's colorful biography, we can assume that these great
enthusiasms have something to do with physical exertion, heroic
efforts, mental tenacity, and a desire to squeeze every drop out of life.

All of us have been acquainted with men who have known the
great enthusiasms, haven't we? Maybe he was our dad. Maybe he
was our uncle or some other relative. Maybe he was a mentor. Oh, he
might not have been President or a Medal of Honor recipient. But in
our eyes, anyway, he was a men of tenacity and a doer who, having
spent himself in a worthy cause, stood triumphant in life's arena. On
the other hand, we've also known some of those cold, timid souls who
have known neither victory nor defeat—men who've known nothing
at all, really, much less the great enthusiasms. The world, after all,
is filled with them.

So what exactly sets these men apart from one another? Why
do some taste—yes, even *live*—the great enthusiasms, while others
know nothing but a life consisting of one cold turkey sandwich after
another?

I would suggest that the difference lies in a fundamental comparison between "existence" and "life." You see, just about everyone has existence—that is, a heart that beats, a pair of lungs that inhale and exhale, and a functioning nervous system. In fact, from the day that you're born until the day that you die, you have existence. But you don't necessarily have *life*.

And the difference between the two kinds of men we're talking about—those who know the great enthusiasms of life and those who know nothing—is the difference between those who exist and those who *live*. It's the difference between squeezing every last drop out of life on the one hand and, on the other, having nothing to squeeze in the first place.

When I think of someone who squeezed everything out of life, I think of my grandfather, Lieutenant Colonel John W. Dillin. Born in 1908, he was a man of many accomplishments and deeds. As a school boy, he was elected mayor of San Diego for a day. (I'm still not sure how he pulled *that* off!) After moving to Florida as a teen, he skipped school and hitch-hiked across the state one day in 1927 to see President Calvin Coolidge. Later, when the Great Depression raged across the country, he persevered and founded the Florida Public Relations Association, one of the leading organizations of its kind in the United States today. Not long after World War 2 erupted, he saw a German submarine torpedo a cargo ship off the Florida coastline (he was director for the St. Augustine chamber of commerce at the time). Partially as a result of that event, he sought and received an officer's commission in the Army Air Forces and went to Europe. His primary job was intelligence, and he frequently executed dangerous bomb-damage reconnaissance missions into enemy territory. Nearly losing his life to German snipers and enemy mines on several occasions, he was awarded the Bronze Star Medal (and that was back when the Bronze Star was still *the Bronze Star*). And because of experiences like these (along with many, many others), did he ever have stories to tell! You knew you were in for a treat whenever he said, "I never will forget the time . . ."

Throughout his life, he always had both hands in one project after another, always taking the lead in organizations and efforts. When he was 88 years old, I remember him saying, "I'm so busy; I'm tired." So I said, "Why don't you quit a lot of this stuff and take it easy?" And he shot back, "Are you crazy? If I did that, I'd be old and dead in six months!" Actually, he was dead about six months later—but not before we squeezed in 9 holes of golf within weeks of his passing. When he died, I was sad but not devastated. After all, he had squeezed every drop out of life, and, in so doing, he left a legacy for us all.

Army Rangers also know the great enthusiasms. For them, the cornerstone of their accomplishments lies partly in the phrase from the Ranger Creed that says, "I will always endeavor." Rangers simply don't know the meaning of the word quit, or in their own language they simply say, "Surrender is not a Ranger word." Likewise, a Ranger who lives his Creed will also follow these words: "I will shoulder more than my share of the task, whatever it may be, one-hundred percent and then some." And that's why Rangers lead the way—because they always endeavor and pour themselves completely into whatever task they find.

A Life that Always Endeavors

But there's more to success in life than blood, sweat, tears, and hard work. In fact, I've known many Rangers over the years who have worked hard and endeavored passionately only to miss out on something of exceptionally greater value. They've missed out on the life that only God can give.

Jesus talked about that life in John 10:10 when he said, "I have come that they might have life and that they might have it abundantly." In so doing, he talked about a life filled with peace and righteousness—not unlike the life that we discussed in the chapter about life navigation. It's a life that comes through faith in God and not primarily through the sweat from a man's brow and the calluses on his hands. Yet, a man who truly finds life in Jesus Christ will do well to endeavor and pursue the great enthusiasms that the great men have known.

I've found over the years that many men often misunderstand the relationship between the endeavors required to succeed and the faith in God that leads to real life. On the one hand, some men focus almost entirely on hard work and reaching for the brass ring of professional, physical, and material success, but they largely leave God out of their life's calculus. On the other hand, some men have a deep and abiding faith, but they just don't see the value in ardently pursuing success and endeavoring greatly. At the end of the day, neither man comprehends the best that God has to offer.

I would argue that real success in life occurs when a man possesses a vibrant and enduring faith in God as well as a passion to pursue the great enthusiasms of manhood and life. But how does a man embrace both, and what exactly does that look like? We might consider as an example the title of a small book written by Theodore Roosevelt near the end of his life, *Fear God and Take Your Own Part*. In that volume, Roosevelt first and foremost urged his readers to have a deep faith in God. Yet he also strongly argued men to take responsibility for themselves and for others through effort and toil, adding a necessary word about the man who shirks that responsibility:

> *Fear God, in the true sense of the word, means love God, respect God, and honor God. . . . In addition to fearing God, it is necessary that we should be able and ready to take our own part. The man who cannot take his own part is a nuisance in the community and a source of weakness.*[2]

Roosevelt wasn't the only man who has touched upon the relationship between faith in God and a man's responsibility to work hard and always endeavor. For example, Oliver Cromwell many years ago told his soldiers, "Trust in the Lord and keep your gunpowder dry" (not bad advice for Rangers, I might add). More recently, Adrian Rogers humorously said, "God provides food for the birds, but he doesn't throw it in the nest."[4] For each of these men, there was a balance between faith in God and, what some might call "an honest day's work" of which any man can be proud.

In this chapter, we're going to look at that balance. Along the way, I'm going to dig deep into my own life's experiences to illustrate that balance and relationship. You see, as a young man and new believer in Jesus Christ, God began to teach me how to trust him deeply and endeavor with energy and ambition to achieve my goals in such a way that would honor him. We'll also highlight some of the fundamentals that go into a strong work ethic. Then we'll focus on the important role that worship and faith ought to have in every man's life.

Hard Work: I Will Always Endeavor

In January 1998, the world saw a true manifestation of desire, determination, and guts. John Elway and the Denver Broncos were playing Brett Favre and the Green Bay Packers in Super Bowl XXXII, and Elway was absolutely determined to win his first Super Bowl. At the start of the third quarter, the game was tied 17-17. Late in the quarter, after a Green Bay punt put Denver on its own 8 yard line, the Broncos began what would turn out to be a 92-yard touchdown drive to take the lead. And the defining moment of both the drive and the game—and perhaps of Elway's entire career—took place on a 3rd-and-6 situation inside the Packers' 20-yard line. Elway took the snap, dropped back, and, as the pocket collapsed, decided to run. As he charged through the defensive line and dove for a first down, he was hit hard and spun around in the air like a helicopter blade. (In fact, that play is now known in NFL lore as "the Helicopter".) After crashing to the ground 8 yards past the line of scrimmage, Elway energetically picked up his 37-year-old body and ran back to the huddle for the next play, which saw the touchdown he so desperately wanted. And roughly 15 minutes later, he had his very first Super Bowl in the bag. It was one of the most exciting Super Bowls ever played, and his effort, in the minds of everyone who saw it, was a true demonstration of desire, tenacity, and win-at-all-costs bravery.

Elway's exploits on the field that night represent the very best of what it means to want something badly, to work hard for it, and to stand on the field of life victorious and triumphant. It's the stuff that real men are made of.

It's also the stuff that Rangers are made of.

The Road to Hard Work

If you don't mind, I'd like to share just a little bit from my own story as an illustration of how this all works. As a boy, I admired the results of hard work and I wanted to taste the fruits of victory. But I never really understood the labor that went into those results. For example, I played drums for several years, and I marveled at the skills of guys like Neil Peart (probably the greatest rock-and-roll drummer of all time) or the kid I met one summer who could play the drums like a pro. But it never really clicked in my mind that abilities like those only come with hours and hours of diligent practice. Likewise, when playing baseball, I admired the skills of those guys who could really connect with that ball and send it over the fence. But it just never occurred to me that it took hard work, desire, and dedication to have a decent batting average. (Mine, by the way, was in the basement.) And I admired the kids who made straight As in school, but I honestly didn't realize that it took hard work and discipline to achieve those kinds of grades. In school, I was happy with a B average (since you got a discount on your car insurance with a B average) and doing just enough to get by beyond that.

I hate to admit it, but I was a quitter, too. When things got tough, I would often pull up my anchor and sail off to something else. Oh, and I was also intimidated by challenges. Many times when a challenging opportunity to excel would present itself, I would run the other way.

Then I decided to join the Marines when I graduated from high school, and that's when things began to change a little bit. First, I had to go to boot camp at a place called Parris Island—and there was no option to quit. Later, as an infantryman on the line, I began to learn a little bit about hard work and the rigors that precede rewards. But I was still just getting by. I really wasn't reaching for the brass ring, and I was still letting challenges intimidate me.

Now, I've always been a reader, and at that time I was reading a few books about the first and second world wars. And as I read through that broad sweep of history, I noticed something. I began to see the same names appear in both wars (Patton, Rommel, MacArthur, to name a few) yet with different ranks. In other words, I began to see that the men who were great generals in World War 2 were fantastic lieutenants, captains, and majors in World War 1. Then, as best I could, I began to put two and two together: "There's no way that General Patton could have been so great in World War 2 if Major Patton hadn't been so great in World War 1." It was a watershed moment for me, because I made an application to my own life: "How can I expect to be somebody someday down the road if I'm not getting after it and excelling *now*?" You see, I had always hoped to do something significant in the future, but I was failing to do anything significant in the present. In short, I was operating from some stupid assumptions such as, "I'll get motivated when . . ." or "I'll start doing something once such-and-such happens."

Not long after that, I was having a talk about future opportunities with my company executive officer, Captain Bill Harrop. And there were two significant takeaways from that conversation. First, he said, "Kramer, you have a lot of potential. But I see you right now mostly as an observer. You stand there and watch other people accomplish things, but you don't go after anything yourself." Bang—right between the eyes. (I was amazed that he had me figured out so well.) Second, he said, "Everything you do or fail to do now will follow you around for a long time." Then he took out his service record book and he showed me all of his officer evaluations as well as his college transcript. And he said, "See, it's all right here. And now I'm trying to get into a funded law program, but my partying and mediocre grades in college are preventing me from getting in. They're following me around." When I left his office, I was, for sure, a more enlightened individual.

I thought long and hard about what Captain Harrop told me. And I said to myself, "Yes, I want to excel, and I think I see how I'm going to do it." But there was still a big hurdle to cross: I still had to actually stick my neck out there and go for something big— something that would have otherwise intimidated me. So I chose to go for a meritorious promotion to the rank of corporal.

In the Marines, a young man can sit around and wait eventually to get promoted or he can compete for a meritorious promotion to the next rank (regardless of how long he's held his present rank). It's a real prize to be won and a sure way to advance faster than your peers. But it's not easy—they don't just give them away. I decided it was the challenge I was looking for.

What does a Marine have to do in order to win a meritorious promotion? He has to go through a day-long series of events and come out on top. The day starts off with a physical fitness test (20 pull ups, 80 sit ups, and an 18-minute 3-mile run to get a perfect 300 score) and then moves on to a uniform, wall-locker, and field equipment inspection where the young Marine meticulously prepares and lays out all of his field equipment on his bed in a prescribed scheme. A senior Marine then comes and inspects all of that. Then the young Marine goes out in the parking lot and, given a drill card and a few minutes to prepare himself, he has to march a squad of Marines all over the place while executing the commands on the drill card. After a quick lunch, he then has a round-robin knowledge-oriented test consisting of about twenty stations of three questions each about all sorts of Marine Corps and infantry knowledge. And finally the young Marine stands before a leadership board composed of each company first sergeant as well as the battalion commander. Each member of the board asks a leadership question and the Marine must answer to the best of his ability. Looking back, the whole process sounds like a great and challenging opportunity, but back then I was very intimated by it.

I knew I needed to choose and overcome a challenge to prove something to myself. So I considered the requirements to win a meritorious promotion and said to myself, "If I let this challenge intimidate me now, I'll be running around with my tail tucked between my legs for the rest of my life. But if I go for it and get it, then I'll hopefully establish a precedent for things to come." So in July 1994, I stuck my neck out and said, "I'm going for it." And then I practiced, studied, memorized, and prepared for that promotion competition like nothing before in my entire life. And then the day came, and I gave it my best shot.

Up until the part where I had to march the Marines around the parking lot, there was another guy who was giving me a real run for my money. After the knowledge and leadership boards, however, I felt like I had a good shot at the whole thing—but I had to wait until the next day for the results. It was a long night of waiting, but the next morning my first sergeant called me in to give me the news . . . that I had won the competition! It was a great day, for sure.

And with that win, a series of events started in my life that all went back to my new discovery that rewards only come with hard work. Soon after the promotion board, I won the base pistol championship, took my squad on to win the annual infantry squad competition, and received an award from the base commander. In the words of Gunnery Sergeant Hartman from *Full Metal Jacket*, I felt like I was "born again hard."

The lessons learned in the Marines stayed with me. After getting out of the Marines, I went to college, seminary, did a second master's degree, and finished a Ph.D. with hardly anything below an A in every course. Then, after coming back on active duty as a chaplain, I went to Jumpmaster School, Ranger School, Pathfinder School, and served numerous with the Rangers. Again, it all went back to a simple but profound realization that the rigors of hard work and discipline always precede the rewards of achievement and victory.

Now, please believe me when I say that I'm not trying to blow my own horn here. That will become obvious enough in the second half of this chapter. Rather, I'm just trying to be transparent about this journey that I've been on for over twenty-five years.

Seven Characteristics of Hard Work

Along the way, a simple verse from the Bible became a solid piece of truth in my life: "The plans of the diligent lead surely to plenty" (Proverbs 21:5). When I first discovered those words, I took them to heart and thought, "God takes a man's decision to work hard very seriously." Building upon that verse, I've discovered numerous principles associated with the rigors and rewards of hard work.

1. Hard Work Begins with Desire
2. Hard Work Fears Failure
3. Hard Work Makes Something Happen
4. Hard Work Plays to Its Strengths
5. Hard Work Does Whatever It Takes

6. Hard Work Overcomes Background
7. Hard Work Stays the Course

Each of these characteristics plays an important part in a man's quest for success and achievement. And each of these characteristics requires a great amount of devotion to the task at hand. So let's talk about them.

Hard Work Begins with Desire

If victory begins with hard work, then hard work begins with desire. And if hard work begins with desire, then desire begins with a simple question: "How badly do I want this?"

When planning for a challenging task, this is a question that every man should ask. Of course, as part of the preparation, we've got to assess exactly what this challenge will cost us. And our job is to count that cost over against our desire to achieve the goal. It's a simple yet important part of achieving the rewards.

Consider this passage from the Bible, where Jesus emphasized the importance of planning and counting the cost:

Suppose one of you wants to build a tower. Will he not first sit down and estimate the cost to see if he has enough money to complete it? For if he lays the foundation but is not able to complete it, everyone who sees it will ridicule him, saying, "This fellow began to build but was not able to finish." (Luke 14:28-29)

Obviously, this guy didn't count the cost and he never asked himself, "How badly do I really want to build this tower?" It's obvious that he didn't want it that badly. Otherwise, he would have either done whatever he needed to do to get enough resources for the tower, or he would have planned for a tower that was within his current means.

Rangers are very familiar with counting the cost. Every young man who volunteers to join the Rangers faces a rigorous eight-week assessment and selection program. Before even beginning that process, he must ask himself, "How badly do I want to be a Ranger?" And then throughout that physically and mentally grueling assessment, he must ask himself every single morning, "How badly do I want to be a Ranger?" If the young man doesn't have it settled in his mind that his desire to be a Ranger outweighs whatever hell he will face that day, he'll quit. But show me a young man whose desire to be a Ranger is greater than the pain he'll endure on any given day of assessment and I'll show you a young man who will one day be a Ranger.

Just like the Rangers, any man who reasonably considers the cost of his endeavor and then keeps his eyes on the prize will enjoy success. Those who become distracted will fall by the wayside. It all begins with desire.

Hard Work Fears Failure

If hard work counts the cost of victory, then it also counts the cost of defeat. Have you ever considered that failure (just like success) comes with a price? For example, the cost of failing Ranger School is a one-way ticket out of the Rangers. Or consider the cost of flunking your college courses: you're out the tuition money and you've prolonged your journey toward graduation. And how about the guy who tried to build the tower but couldn't finish? It cost him ridicule and mocking from his neighbors.

For some people—incredibly—failure is not that big of deal. These are the people who just roll along and take whatever life deals them, whether good or bad. Again, remember "tower guy"? I guess he didn't think being the goat of the neighborhood was all that bad.

Now, it's important that we don't become paranoid about failure, because we'll go crazy if we do. Rather, let's just say that those who want to succeed need a very healthy respect for failure. Otherwise, we're opening ourselves up to the possibility of failure, which, in the minds of successful people like Rangers, is simply unacceptable.

Here's an example from personal experience. When I tried out for the Rangers, I was bent on succeeding and I had a real fear of failure. I considered the cost and didn't want to take anything for granted. I also considered the impacts that failure would have. For one thing, my battalion commander at the time was Lieutenant Colonel Frank Jenio, a legend in the Ranger community who, in my opinion, was nothing short of King Leonidas reborn. He was one of my biggest supporters, and letting him down would have been unbearable. Plus, my battalion sergeant major, Command Sergeant Major Bert Puckett, was also a long-time Ranger veteran who used to tell me all the time about his days with the Rangers. And on top of that, my division chaplain, Lieutenant Colonel Matt Goff, formerly served with the Rangers and had high expectations of me. And I didn't want to let my wife and children down, either.

Look at it this way: the fear of failure cuts two ways like a double-edged sword. On the one hand, fear of failure might prevent a man from ever taking up a challenging task in the first place: "If I attempt this or that, I might fail. Therefore, I'm not going to try it at all." In that case, fear of failure can be a paralyzing force that keeps a man from pursuing anything at all. But on the other hand, fear of failure can be the strongest motivation for a man who puts himself out there and goes for something big: "Well, I might have bitten off a bit more than I can easily chew, but failure is not an option for me so I'm going to chew and chew and chew until I've accomplished the task." In that case, fear of failure can be a healthy motivation.

Hard Work Makes Something Happen

One day in Ranger School I was just about to fall asleep in class when the Ranger instructor said, "There are two kinds of people in this world: those who wait for something to happen and those who make something happen." When he said that, I perked up just a little bit and thought, "Now there's a real piece of wisdom. I'm going to write that down."

You know, there's a lot of truth in that statement, and experience confirms to us every day that it's true. There are those who wait for things to happen—who wait for *someone else* to do something. But there are also those who make things happen. They see what needs to be done and they do what needs to be done. They create opportunities rather than wait for opportunities. And, by the way, there's a direct relationship between fearing failure and making stuff happen, because that fear of failure is often what motivates us to make something happen when nothing else seems to be working. Desperate times call for desperate actions, right?

As an example of someone who wants to make something happen rather than waiting for something to happen, consider the noted British writer and theologian, G. K. Chesterton. Someone once asked him, "If you were stranded on a desert island and could only have one book, what would it be?" Everyone assumed Chesterton's answer would be, "The Bible." Instead, Chesterton replied, "Why, *A Practical Guide to Shipbuilding*, of course!"⁵

The difference between making something happen and waiting for something to happen is the basic ability to step outside of your little sphere of existence and to influence, shape, and overcome external circumstances. For instance, a student in Ranger School might find things falling apart all around him as he leads his platoon on a mission—his patrol is lost, some of his guys are falling asleep, the Ranger instructor is harassing him, and so forth. If he doesn't do something to right the ship, he'll possibly fail the school. What does he do? He gets it together and makes something happen. What about the football team that's down by two touchdowns with five minutes left to play? If they're going to win, they've got come together and make something happen. It's just that simple.

A famous story from the Spanish-American War speaks of someone who made something happen in a moment of crisis. Known as "A Message to Garcia" and written by Elbert Hubbard in 1899,[6] the story has to do with a mission to find a Cuban insurgent leader named Garcia whose cooperation was needed in the battle against the Spanish. Here's the gist of the actual story itself:

> *When war broke out between Spain and the United States, it was very necessary to communicate quickly with the leader of the insurgents. Garcia was somewhere in the mountain fastnesses of Cuba—no one knew where. No mail or telegraph could reach him. The President must secure his co-operation, and quickly. What to do! Someone said to the President, "There's a fellow by the name of Rowan who will find Garcia for you, if anybody can." Rowan was sent for and given a letter to be delivered to Garcia. [He] took the letter, sealed it up in an oil-skin pouch, strapped it over his heart, [and] in four days landed by night off the coast of Cuba from an open boat, disappeared into the jungle, and in three weeks came out on the other side of the island, having traversed a hostile country on foot, and having delivered his letter to Garcia.*

The story itself is an amazing tale, but Hubbard's main effort in writing the article is to highlight Rowan's ability to make something happen without delay and without excuse:

> *The point I wish to make is this: McKinley gave Rowan a letter to be delivered to Garcia; Rowan took the letter and did not ask, "Where is he at?" By the Eternal! There is a man whose form*

should be cast in deathless bronze and the statue placed in every college in the land. It is not book-learning young men need, nor instruction about this or that, but a stiffening of the vertebrae which will cause them to be loyal to a trust, to act promptly, concentrate their energies; do the thing—"carry a message to Garcia!"

Civilization is one long anxious search for just such individuals. Anything such a man asks will be granted; his kind is so rare that no employer can afford to let him go. He is wanted in every city, town, and village—in every office, shop, store and factory. The world cries out for such; he is needed, and needed badly—the man who can "Carry a message to Garcia!"

The story highlights the ability of one man to make something happen at the micro level that greatly impacted the macro level. And that story has inspired generations of men to go above and beyond and make something happen in a desperate moment. It's what real men do. It's what Rangers do.

Hard Work Does Whatever It Takes

Remember John Elway and "the Helicopter" play? He was a man backed in a corner who did whatever he had to do in order to make a first down at a crucial moment in the game. He understood that hard work does whatever it takes to accomplish the mission—physically, emotionally, and spiritually.

The old saying that "when the going gets tough, the tough get going" applies here. Yes, every man will sooner or later find himself in a tough situation. That situation might be in life-or-death combat or it might be an episode from some other challenging part of our personal experiences. At the end of the day, a more elite man will find a way to make something happen by doing whatever it takes.

Again, I go back to my own life's experience because I know it better than any other. I started Ranger School in January, fully knowing that my unit was set to deploy in July for 15 months to Iraq. Specifically, I was desperate to go "straight through" because even one recycle would mean an additional month away from my family at Fort Bragg. (Ranger School has three phases, and a student must pass each phase one at a time or repeat the phase over again. Every time a student "re-cycles" a phase, he basically adds another month to his time in Ranger School. I've known a few guys who were in school for six to eight months!) And with that long deployment coming up, I didn't want to spend any more time away from my family than absolutely necessary.

In Ranger School, every student must spend time in a graded leadership position. Usually this means either being in charge of planning a mission and giving the mission briefing to the rest of the platoon in the unit area or being in charge of actually executing the mission in the woods. While in a leadership position, the students is graded by the instructors. Based on his performance in that leadership position, he gets a "GO" or a "NO GO."

Well, I got my GO in the first phase and then moved onto the second phase in the north-Georgia mountains. The instructors put me in charge of planning the mission and briefing the plan to my fellow students. I was bent on getting my GO right then and there and was ready to do whatever I had to do. We began our planning late in the evening and instructors told us that we had to plan the mission, pack our equipment, and get a couple hours of sleep before the mission brief early the next morning. We had about 6 hours to make all of that happen (and maybe get a little sleep). Since I was in charge of planning that evening and also briefing the mission the next morning, I wanted everything to be just right. We conducted the majority of our planning and packed our gear. After doing all of that, we had a few hours to sleep. But while the rest of the platoon took advantage of that time sleeping, I thought about what was on the line for me. We were all dead tired and I desperately wanted to get some sleep, but I knew that if I gave a solid briefing in the morning then I would get my GO. So I did what I had to do: I went into the latrine and wrote out my entire plan and rehearsed how I would brief the mission in the morning. No sleep for me, but I was desperate to get my GO and I was willing to do what I had to do.

When the next morning came, everyone took their place in the bleachers in the planning hut, and I got up and gave the order. At the time I was a chaplain, so when I got up to give the order, I didn't pitch it—I *preached* it. I even got a resounding "Amen" from my guys when I talked about shooting the "enemy" in the face! Everything went just like I had planned, and then the instructor said to me, "That was the best mission briefing I've heard in two years here." I knew I had my GO.

I'm sure you're beginning to see how these principles are interrelated. Desire and drive go hand in hand with a fear of failure. And the desperate times that are often created by a fear of failure give rise to a "make-something-happen-no-matter-what" work ethic. In other words, a more elite man will pay his dues, endure the rigors, and taste the rewards.

Hard Work Plays to Its Strengths

What are your strengths and what are your weaknesses? What are you good at, and what do you need to work on? If you plan on succeeding in life, you'll need to know these things—and you'll need to play to your strengths. Playing to your strengths requires an understanding of your personality. Psychologists call this "self awareness" or sometimes "emotional intelligence," and getting a handle on it is oftentimes a life-long process.

Why is it important to know your strengths and play to them?

Because no one is good at *everything*. We all have our strengths and weaknesses. The key is to play to our strengths and engage in those things that we're good at.

A great example of this is the story of David and Goliath from the Bible. David was a young shepherd boy, who, along with the entire Israelite army, faced a giant named Goliath. No one was man enough to go after Goliath, so David announced that he would take him on. The Israelite king, a man named Saul, thought that it would be a good idea to outfit David with his own armor and battle kit (understanding, of course, that David was too small to wear and use Saul's equipment). This is how the story unfolded:

> *Then Saul dressed David in his own tunic. He put a coat of armor on him and a bronze helmet on his head. David fastened on his sword over the tunic and tried walking around in them. "I cannot go in these," he said to Saul, "because I am not used to them." So he took them off. Then he took his staff in his hand, chose five smooth stones from the stream, put them in his pouch, and with his sling in his hand he approached the giant. (1 Samuel 17:38-40)*

The rest of the story is history: Goliath mocked David for being so small and for coming to him with such meager weapons, David took one stone in his sling and knocked Goliath out with a head shot, and then he went over and cut Goliath's head off with the giant's own sword.

The key takeaway here is that David knew his strengths and he played to them. He didn't try to be someone he wasn't; he didn't try to do something he wasn't good at doing. Rather, he fought the battle with the abilities that he had. And that's exactly what hard work does on the way to victory and success—it knows its powers and limitations and fights the battle accordingly.

Do you know who you are? Do you know your strengths and

weaknesses? Do you know your personality type and how that type interacts with others? Without a decent grasp on these kinds of things, you're not going into battle properly equipped. After all, you can't live at giant levels without taking on giant challenges. But how can you adequately face those giant problems without knowing the strengths that will help you succeed?

Maybe you've been in a job at some point in time where you felt like you had to be awesome at every aspect of your job. Maybe you assumed that your supervisor expected you to be awesome at every aspect of your job. That's how I felt when I first showed up to work as a chaplain with the Rangers. I thought I needed to be Superman at everything under the sun, and for the better part of six months I knocked myself out trying to be awesome at everything. But then I realized that I could excel overall if I leveraged my strengths in the areas where I was really gifted and at least met a minimum standard in the areas where I wasn't especially talented. That was a huge revelation for me and I went on to have a pretty successful run working with those Rangers.

Hard Work Overcomes Background

I might also add that hard work overcomes background. And just what does that mean? It means that regardless of where you're from, how much money your parents made, what kind of educational opportunities you were afforded, and the color of your skin, you can climb the ladder of life through hard work. In fact, there's every reason to believe that, through hard work, you can climb higher than someone who had a more privileged childhood and upbringing. Consider what Proverbs says:

> *A servant who acts wisely will rule over a son who acts shamefully, and will share in the inheritance with the brothers.* (Proverbs 17:2)

That's an important truth from the Bible, not least because it highlights personal decisions and the ability of anyone—regardless of their background—to "make good" in life. So, no more excuses and reasons for being held back. Go forth and do likewise!

This is one of the reasons I love working with Rangers. They live by standards, period. Either a man meets the Ranger standard or he doesn't. They don't care where you were born, who your parents were, the color of your skin, or the sound of your last name. They only want to know one thing: can you perform? If so, you're in and you're a Ranger. If not, they'll kick you to the curb in a skinny second. It's as simple as that. And it's a great illustration of life. At the end of the day, you can't ride your parents' coat-tails or bank on your family name. You've got to make your own way through endeavoring without excuses. That's how a more elite man lives his life.

Hard Work Stays the Course

One more thing: hard work stays the course—that is, hard work endures. And hard work realizes that the daily grind is really the daily climb. That is, success is rarely found in an overnight delivery package. Rather, true success is accomplished by laying one brick at a time, day by day by day, in the structure of your life. Or, at least in one case, success comes one rail at a time.

If you want an amazing example of hard work and endurance, read Stephen Ambrose's book, *Nothing Like It In the World*, the story about building the transcontinental railroad in the 1860s.[7] It's an incredible story of how hundreds of engineers and thousands of laborers accomplished what was, up to that time, the most amazing feat of engineering construction the world had ever seen. Two companies, the Central Pacific Railroad and the Union Pacific Railroad, began racing toward a common point of connection. Day by day, they cleared the grade; day by day they laid the rails. On the Nebraska plains, they sometimes laid as much as 4 miles of track in a day, some days they laid as little as 500 yards. But they laid it day by day. In the mountains of California and Utah, they blasted their way through solid rock foot by foot by single foot. But they blasted day by day. All in all, it was a monumental task. And, they realized success in the end because they went to work and persevered, day by day by day.

Every Ranger knows that the trajectory of success is a line that connects one day to the next, and that the line climbs higher and higher as long as it remains unbroken. In other words, when the line is broken—when a Ranger says, "I quit," or he does something stupid, selfish, or cowardly—the trajectory ceases its climb to the heights of victory. So keep the line connected and don't give up on the challenges that you face.

Surrender is not a Ranger word, right?

Hard Work: Only One Side of the Coin

OK, anyone out there in favor of hard work and the rewards that it brings? Hopefully we've been able to highlight some of the important characteristics of hard work. I'm sure you've recognized most of them.

But don't forget that success is like a two-sided coin. Hard work and endeavoring to achieve a victory is only one side of that coin. The other side is an abiding and enduring faith in God. In the next section, we're going to see why faith and worship are so vitally important in the life of a more elite man—and why a one-sided coin is dangerous. So pay attention.

Faith: The Second Side of the Coin

A more elite man concerns himself with more than just effort and accomplishment. In fact, his priority isn't on advancing in this world, per se. Rather, a more elite man puts God above all other things in his life. That means that nothing else takes God's place. A more elite man acknowledges that everything he is and ever hopes to be ultimately comes from God. And, last but not least, a more elite man measures his worth, success, and significance according to God's yardstick and not his own. And when he does, he will find more joy, happiness, and fulfillment than he ever could from achievements alone.

The Source of Success

The importance of faith and worship is that they remind us of the source of our strength that allows us to work hard. You may remember when I told you my own story of hard work and how I said that I wasn't trying to blow my own horn. You see, at about the same time that I was chasing after that meritorious promotion, God brought to my attention a very important verse from the Bible. It's a simple statement that carries huge weight for all of those who would work hard to achieve goals:

> *A man can receive nothing unless it has been given to him from Heaven.* (John 3:27)

When I read that verse, I began to see that I could not receive a single, solitary thing apart from God's gracious and merciful hand. Of course, I knew that my hard work wasn't in vain, since God takes our decisions and efforts very seriously. But I did begin to understand that all that I have comes from God. So as I jumped over each hurdle on the way to my meritorious promotion, I quietly said to myself, "A man can receive nothing unless it has been given to him from Heaven." And, when going for the base pistol championship, every time I raised my pistol and pulled the trigger, I reminded myself, "A man can receive nothing unless it has been given to him from

Heaven." And every time I made an "A" in college and beyond, I said, "A man can receive nothing unless it has been given to him from Heaven." You see, it really has become a key verse in my life.

Now, building upon the wisdom of John 3:27, check out this passage in the Bible where God reminds his people that he is the ultimate source of their successes:

You may say to yourself, "My power and the strength of my hands have produced this wealth for me." But remember the Lord your God, for it is he who gives you the ability to produce wealth, and so confirms his covenant, which he swore to your forefathers, as it is today. (Deuteronomy 8:17-18)

Again, it's not that I'm trying to discount all that I've already said about hard work. Rather, I'm just trying to put it all into perspective— into God's perspective, that is. And that's a very important thing, because forgetting God and his provision only leads to heartache, chaos, and sadness.

So don't be like that British soldier who puffed out his chest and said to Winston Churchill: "I am a self-made man." In response, Churchill replied, "Congratulations; you have just relieved God of a very solemn responsibility."[8] And I might add that many other great men of history have shared this perspective.

Abraham Lincoln, in the throes of the great Civil War, issued a proclamation appointing a national day of fasting and prayer in March 1863. In so doing, he encouraged Americans everywhere to remember the source of their good blessings and prosperity—and he warned them against an ungrateful attitude toward God in response. Consider these words carefully:

We have been preserved these many years in peace and prosperity, we have grown in numbers, wealth and power as no other nation has ever grown, but we have forgotten the gracious hand that has preserved us in peace and has multiplied, enriched, and strengthened us; and we have vainly imagined in the deceitfulness of our hearts that all these blessings were produced by some superior wisdom and virtue of our own. Intoxicated now with unbroken success, we have become too self-sufficient to feel the necessity of redeeming and persevering grace, too proud to pray to the God that made us.[9]

Good stuff for all of us. And while the language may be a bit flowery and melodramatic, the principle and intent is right on target.

So remember God in the midst of your triumph. Don't take all the credit for yourself while leaving his divine mercy out in the cold. Otherwise, you'll have an imbalanced life.

The God Priority

Faith and worship not only remind us of the source of our successes, but they also remind us that there is a spiritual priority to life and success in life. In other words, we need to remember that there are some things more important than human effort, toil, and accomplishment.

I'm reminded of the story in the Bible about the two sisters, Mary and Martha, who had Jesus over as a guest one day. Here's how the story unfolded:

Jesus came to a village where a woman named Martha opened her home to him. She had a sister named Mary, who sat at the Lord's feet and listened to what he said. But Martha was distracted by all the preparations that had to be made. So she came to him and asked, "Lord, don't you care that my sister has left me to do the work all by myself? Tell her to help me!"

But the Lord answered, "Martha, Martha, you are worried and upset about many things, but only one thing is needed. Mary has chosen what is best, and it will not be taken away from her." (Luke 10:38-42)

There's so much that we could say about this story and about the spiritual priority principle. Like the last section about the source of our success, this section is not meant to discount hard work and courageous efforts. But, again, I'm trying to put it all into perspective. For Jesus himself said that there are some things that are more important than hard work, whether in his response to Martha, in his words to his disciples in Matthew 16:26: "What should it profit a man if he should gain the whole world, but lose his soul?" Or what about his story about the hard-working business man who forgot about God:

The ground of a certain rich man produced a good crop. He thought to himself, "What shall I do? I have no place to store my crops." Then he said, "This is what I will do. I will tear down my barns and build bigger barns, and there I will store all of my goods. And I'll say to myself, 'You have plenty of good things laid up for many years. Take life easy; eat, drink, and be merry.'" But God said to him, "You fool! This very night your life will be demanded from you. Then who will get what you have prepared for yourself?" This is how it will be with anyone who stores up things for himself but is not rich toward God. (Luke 12:16-21)

Does Jesus condemn hard work? Not at all. Does Jesus say that this man shouldn't have been diligent in business? No way! But, again, he says that there are some things more important than hard work, diligence, and material success. Jeremiah the prophet likewise touched on this God priority:

This is what the Lord says: Let not the wise man boast of his wisdom or the strong man boast of his strength or the rich man boast of his riches, but let him who boasts boast about this: that he understands and knows me. (Jeremiah 9:23-24)

In fact, every challenge in life requires a spiritual priority if real success is to be achieved. In the aftermath of World War 2, for instance, even as the ink was drying on the surrender documents signed by the Japanese, General Douglas MacArthur sensed that true peace and post-war success demanded a spiritual priority. Consider carefully these words from his radio speech following the Japanese surrender on the deck of the battleship *U.S.S. Missouri*:

Today the guns are silent [and] a new era is upon us. Even the lesson of victory itself brings with it profound concern, both for our future security and the survival of civilization. The destructiveness of the war potential, through progressive advances in scientific discovery, has in fact now reached a point which revises the traditional concept of war.

We have had our last chance. If we do not now devise some greater and more equitable system, Armageddon will be at our door. The problem is basically theological and involves a spiritual [revival] and improvement of the human character that will synchronize with our almost matchless advances in science . . . and all material and cultural development of the past two thousand years. It must be of the spirit if we are to save the flesh.[10]

You know, whether you're trying to pave the way for world peace or you're simply trying to make your way as a man in this world, there is a profound truth in MacArthur's words. And that truth is that human effort, apart from a spiritual emphasis and priority, is ultimately a part of the problem rather than the solution.

Remember, there are *two* sides to a life well lived.

Goals are Not the Ultimate Goal

Men are goal oriented by nature, and Rangers may just be the most goal-oriented men of them all. But with that pursuit of goals comes a danger. And that danger amounts to a tendency to define one's identity and worth in terms of achievement and accomplishment without any other consideration. Or, in other words, men become enamored with accomplishing goals simply for the sake of accomplishing goals. And the end result is that achievement is the measure of all things meaningful—that is, men even begin to find their *identity* in their accomplishments. It's a subtle trap into which many men, and many Rangers, fall.

Patrick Morley puts his finger on this very issue as he points out the pitfalls related to the accomplishment of goals simply for the sake of accomplishment:

> *One of the gripping problems men face is that achieving becomes an unrelated string of hollow victories. That's the problem with goals: you have to keep setting new ones because achieving them doesn't provide lasting satisfaction.*[11]

Of course, Morley is not criticizing setting goals or accomplishing them. But he does try to put all things into the proper perspective. And that perspective says that we cannot allow ourselves ultimately to seek personal, emotional, and spiritual validation through victory itself.

Why is this a danger? Well, when you get your sense of significance and identity from accomplishment, as Morley says, you've got to keep winning, achieving, and reaching for the next rung on the ladder to maintain your sense of worth. This works well, as long as you can keep it up. But what happens when you don't reach a goal you've set? And what if you need to "take a knee" and rest? You'll lose your sense of significance.

When I was a little boy, the 1981 movie *Chariots of Fire* took America by storm. It was based on the true story of two British track stars, Harold Abrahams and Eric Liddell, competing in the 1924 Olympics. It provides a great lesson on the very issue that we're discussing. Liddell was a gifted athlete who ran ultimately for God's glory; Abrahams, likewise a very talented athlete, ran ultimately for his own glory. Liddell's ultimate goal was missionary service in China, but he devoted long hours to training for the Olympics. His sister one day questioned his priorities, and he answered, "Jennie, Jennie, you've got to understand. I believe God made me for a purpose—for China. But he also made me fast! And when I run, *I feel his pleasure.*" On the other hand, just before running his final race, Abrahams lamented to his friend, "I'm twenty-four years old and I've never known contentment. I'm forever in pursuit, and I don't even know what it is I'm chasing. In a moment, I will raise my eyes and look down that corridor, 4 feet wide, with 10 lonely seconds to justify my whole existence. But will I?"[12]

Wow. The contrast between the two men's perspectives could not be more pronounced. Patrick Morley comments on the two men in this way: "Both men won a gold medal, but one won the medal for himself, while the other won his medal for God." And then Morley asks, "Do you feel God's pleasure in what you do or, like Abrahams, does contentment elude you?"

Here's another example, this time from the NFL. A few years ago, during Super Bowl week, I saw a series of interviews on ESPN with former Super Bowl coaches and players. Two of the interviews particularly grabbed my attention. One was with Bud Grant, former coach of the Minnesota Vikings in the 1970s and early 1980s; the other was with Fran Tarkington, who played quarterback for Grant in Minnesota. As NFL history buffs will remember, during those years the Vikings went to the Super Bowl four times—and lost all four times. What the two men said couldn't have been more opposite. When asked if not winning a Super Bowl was hard to think about, Tarkington said, "It's like a weight hung around my neck. My life has been consumed by negative emotions about it." On the other hand, when Grant was asked the same question, he said, "It would have been nice to win a Super Bowl, but I don't think my life would be any better than it is right now."[13] Obviously, Bud Grant has defined who he is and his sense of significance at a level beyond his list of accomplishments and achievements, while Tarkington has struggled to define himself apart from 4 football games that he lost (a mere 4 hours of game time out of his entire life).

Now, how does God figure into all of this? And if goals are not the ultimate goal, then what is? Well, Jesus once got into a conversation with a *very* successful lawyer, and the lawyer basically asked Jesus to define the most important pursuit in life. And how did Jesus respond? He said, "Love the Lord your God with all of your heart, with all of your soul, with all of your mind, and with all of your strength. And love your neighbor as yourself" (Mark 12:28-34). When the lawyer heard that, he affirmed it by saying that loving God and loving your neighbor is more important than "all burnt offerings and sacrifices."

That's a very important conversation for our purposes in two significant ways. First, Jesus defined life's ultimate pursuit in terms that are *not quantifiable*. And what do I mean by that? I mean to say that life's ultimate pursuit is a way of life rather than a rung on the ladder of success. (Consider that even the lawyer saw the importance of Jesus' response over a large quantity of "offerings and sacrifices"). Second, Jesus' response tells us that real success in life comes from focusing on others and the needs of others rather than on accomplishments that enhance and build our own esteem and resume. Or, as Patrick Morley writes in *The Man in the Mirror*, "Significance [in life] is not possible unless what we do contributes to the welfare of other people."[14]

The Real Yardstick

So how do we as men measure our life's worth and who we are? Do we ultimately measure ourselves by our own accomplishments and hard work? Or do we use a different yardstick at the end of the day?

Some people do measure who they are in terms of what they're able to achieve by the sweat of their brow and the calluses on their hands. These are the people who revel in the human spirit of conquest, enlightenment, and progress—the ability to pull themselves up by their own bootstraps. These are also the people who set up for themselves homemade rules for things like morality and meaning. Historically, the word "humanism" has been a broad umbrella term under which these kinds of people like to congregate. And what is humanism? Humanism is basically the view that mankind establishes its own moral and ideological values apart from the influence of a god, and that mankind determines its destiny wholly apart from any idea of a god.

Probably the best example of the humanist spirit is the poem *Invictus*, written over 100 years ago by William Ernest Henley:

Out of the night that covers me,
Black as a Pit from pole to pole,
I thank whatever gods may be,
For my unconquerable soul.

In the fell clutch of circumstance,
I have not winced nor cried aloud.
Under the bludgeoning of chance,
My head is bloody, but unbowed.

Beyond this place of wrath and tears,
Looms but the Horror of the shade,
And yet the menace of the years,
Finds and shall find me unafraid.

It matters not how strait the gate,
How charged with punishment the scroll.
I am the master of my fate.
I am the captain of my soul.[15]

On the surface, there's something admirable about this poem, isn't there? After all, a man can very much appreciate the determination to succeed, to overcome challenging circumstances, and to face fear with courage. But one thing in this poem is tragically missing: God. Henley vaguely refers to the "gods"—if they even exist—but then he shakes his fist in the air, stands on the top of his man-made mountain of human effort and reason and says, "*I* am the master of my fate; *I* am the captain of my soul."

I'd say it sounds more like he's on thin ice!

If life is like a coin, Henley's coin shines brightly on one side, but he allows the other side of his coin to become tarnished beyond recognition. It's really a sad state of affairs.

Fear God and Take Your Own Part: A Balancing Act

A more elite man loves God with all his heart, soul, mind, and strength. He also always endeavors to go beyond the average and make the most of the life that God has given to him. He lives by the principles of both John 3:27 ("A man can receive nothing unless it has been given to him from Heaven") and Proverbs 21:5 ("The plans of the diligent lead surely to plenty").

If there was ever someone who personified the blend of these two themes, I would have to name the great eighteenth-century British preacher John Wesley. Although short in stature—he was only about 5' 2" tall—he was a powerful force for God, a man who, in fact, shook and took two continents for Jesus Christ. He was a man of great devotion, worship, and faith, but he was also a man who knew the value of hard work and diligence. Over the course of his life, he preached over 40,000 sermons, worked in 15 different languages, and wrote over 600 pieces of literature. At the age of 83, he became angry with his doctor who told him to preach no more than 14 times a week! At the age of 86, he wrote in his journal, "Laziness is slowly creeping in; there is an increasing tendency to stay in bed past 5:30 in the morning." He was the paragon of hard work and effort. Yet, when he died, at his request, these words were inscribed on his gravestone at Aldersgate, England: "Reader, if you feel constrained to praise the instrument, stop and give God the glory."[16]

A more elite man lives his life at that level. He knows the great enthusiasms and strives valiantly in pursuit of them. Yet he lives for much more than accomplishment alone. He does not make his boast in his efforts, courage, and victories. Rather, he makes his boast in nothing except the fact that he knows God personally.

5

My Care of Equipment: Financial Wisdom in a Foolish World

A key phrase in the Ranger Creed is, "My care of equipment shall set the example for others to follow." While a Ranger's equipment is limited mostly to military items such as weapons, ammunition, mission-essential electronics, rucksacks, and such, the principle of maintain positive control of and wisely using the resources that God has given has a much broader application. In both cases—a Ranger's equipment or the resources we possess as men—the commander's intent for those items is paramount.

Men today need to get wise regarding their money, possessions, and resources. Too many are deep in debt, spending like there's no tomorrow, or selfish with what they have. God expects better from those to whom he has given so much, and he wants to bless those who honor him with all that they have.

In this chapter we're going to first talk about some wise perspectives on money and possessions that will establish a foundation for everything else you do with your stuff. Then we're going to talk about some practical principles for using your stuff.

Some Perspectives on Money and Possessions

A man's beliefs about money and material possessions will largely determine how he uses those things. So it's important that we have the right perspectives on our cash and on our stuff. Otherwise, we're going to discover that we don't own our things but that our things own us!

Could that be said of you? Do you use your money, or does your money use you? Do you own your things, or do your things own you? Here's a little test that might show you some leaks in your financial boat:

1. **Debt Percentage**. Do you spend more than 35% of your monthly income on paying off debt (cars, credit cards, house, etc)? Many financial experts say that, for the average person, a debt load of more than 35% is too much.

2. **Daily Expenses**. Do you have to dig into your savings to pay for daily or monthly expenses such as gas for your car or other fixed expenses? That might indicate that you've got a weak or non-existent budget—or that you're living beyond your means.

3. **Debt Awareness**. Are you in "Fuzzy-ville" when it comes to your debts? In other words, do you know exactly how much you owe and to whom? A good test is to try to list all of your debts (how much and name of each lender) in 60 seconds or less. If you can't do it, then chances are you've got too much debt.

4. **Bill Collectors**. Do you have bill collectors calling you and harassing you about unpaid bills? This is a real red flag, and it shows convincingly that you're in bondage to your money and possessions.

5. **Integrity**. Have you ever been (or considered being) dishonest about money in order to get more? Have you ever done something dishonest at work in order to get money that wasn't rightfully yours? Again, this is a core issue that points to a much larger problem than dollars and cents.

OK, how did you do on the test? It's not the be-all, end-all index, but your answers will reasonable illustrate your financial stability. Sometimes we try to ignore the kinds of issues listed above, choosing rather to bury our financial heads in the sand, hoping that the problems will just go away. But these are definitely NOT the kinds of problems that resolve themselves—they need our deliberate attention.

As we've already said, many of these issues can be traced back to perspectives we have about money and possessions. So let's get a financial azimuth check by discussing some of these basic perspectives.

The True Source of Wealth

Where does money come from, and how do we get it in the first place? Does it just fall from the sky? (Men everywhere wish it was that simple!) Or is there a more down-to-earth explanation for the wealth we have in our bank accounts? Consider the following verses from the Bible:

A man can receive nothing unless it has been given to him from Heaven. (John 3:27)

What do you have that you did not receive from God? (1 Corinthians 4:7)

Don't say to yourself, "My power and the strength of my hands have produced this wealth for me." But remember the Lord your

God, for it is he who gives you the ability to do work and produce wealth. (Deuteronomy 8:17-18)

These verses and others like them from the Bible speak of (1) origin and (2) ownership.

First, they remind us very clearly that what we possess (and even life itself) has been given to us from God. This is no small thing, mostly because it then directs us toward an attitude of humble thanksgiving and gratitude for what we have. Consider the fact that the holiday of Thanksgiving, whether you realize it or not, is all about God. After all, if we're giving thanks for something, then we're giving thanks to Someone for that something—right? The noted British writer G. K. Chesterton framed it this way: "If my children wake up on Christmas morning and have somebody to thank for putting candy into their stocking, have I no one to thank for putting two feet into mine?"[1]

You see, an attitude of humility and thanksgiving gives us pause when we choose what to do with our money and possessions. It prevents us from making hasty and impulse-driven decisions, and it reminds us of a greater good and higher purpose behind all we have and possess.

Second, these verses remind us of ownership—that is, they remind us that ultimately what we have doesn't really belong to us. Even though we're in possession of it, it nevertheless really belongs to God. (No, in this case "possession is 9/10 of the law" doesn't apply!) Sometimes we hear the word "stewardship" used in connection with wealth and resources. What is stewardship? It's basically the idea that we're to take care of something that belongs to someone else, and that we're to use those materials and resources according to the wishes of the rightful owner. Like the view of origin and the humble attitude that it promotes, a proper perspective on what we have and possess—namely, that God is the rightful owner of it all—gives us humility that helps us wisely use our wealth. As we will see in a moment, there's a fast-paced attitude towards wealth in our world today that shouts words like "NOW!" and "MORE!" and "MUST HAVE." But humility about wealth and possessions trumps that primal urge to accumulate above and beyond common sense and helps us to make wise decisions.

The True Measure of Wealth

How does one truly measure wealth? Do we add up all that we have and determine our "net worth" and the value of our overall portfolio? Do we define our worth according to certain financial or material milestones achieved? How about the toys and things that we've accumulated—do they determine who we are and what we're worth? There's certainly a hustle machine out there that tries to talk us into measuring our life's worth by all of these things.

But it's a terrible mistake to buy into that line.

What is it that you're really hoping to "get" in the next year? Maybe you've been telling yourself, "If I can just buy one of those, I'll really be happy!" Unfortunately, the idea that accumulation can bring happiness has not delivered the goods promised. Research, experience, and the examples of other people tell us that accumulating and consuming more stuff doesn't bring true happiness and lasting riches.

Recently, the New Economic Foundation in London published what they call "The Happy Planet Index." The index basically measured the relationship between a nation's rate of consumption (that is, how much and how quickly they bought and accumulated stuff) and its overall quality of life:

If consuming more made people happier, then a country's Gross Domestic Product (GDP), a traditional measurement of national success, would reflect the nation's happiness. But it didn't. Just ask the people of the tiny South Pacific island nation of Vanuatu. According to the Index, they are the happiest people in the planet in terms happiness and life expectancy—even though its GDP was ranked 207 out of 233 countries. Unlike the simple country of Vanuatu, the tech-heavy countries did not fare well. Germany takes 81ˢᵗ place, Japan is 95ᵗʰ, and the United States comes in at 150ᵗʰ.[2]

So what does this say? It shows us that stuff doesn't bring meaningful, lasting happiness, no matter how much we think it might. It also means that we often look like suckers when we foolishly assume, "If I can just buy a _____, then I'll be happy" (fill in the blank with whatever you want).

Without realizing it, many people try to find their true wealth and worth in financial or material milestones, only to be eventually disappointed when they finally reach that milestone. Aren't we all guilty of this from time to time? As an illustration, my wife worked at a car dealership while she was in college, and a salesman came to work one day with a mile-wide smile on his face. She said, "Why are you so happy today?" He said, "I've finally 'arrived.' I just bought a Lexus!"

So how are you measuring your true wealth and worth? It's a subtle temptation in our world to use a financial or material yardstick, isn't it? Consider the words of John Bogle, founder of the Vanguard Group, one of the world's leading investment companies:

What are the things by which we should measure our lives? I'm still searching for the ultimate answer to that question. But I know that we can never let things as such—material possessions we may come to accumulate—become the measure of our lives. In a nation as rich with material abundance as ours, it is an easy trap to fall into. Some say "man is the measure of all things." Today, I fear, we are becoming a society in which "things are the measure of the man."[3]

Those are some great insights from a man who has more money than all of us multiplied by 1,000 will ever have in our entire lives. In other words, if there's anyone on the face of the earth who could *legitimately* measure his life and worth in monetary and material terms, it would be John Bogle. But he has evidently discovered the foolishness of doing that—and, hopefully, we can learn the same lesson.

So if getting stuff for the purpose of having it, flaunting it, and using it to measure our lives isn't the true purpose of wealth, then why have it at all? What is the true purpose of wealth?

Primarily, wealth is to facilitate our survival. After all, it costs money to eat, put clothes on our backs, and transport ourselves from point A to point B. But beyond that, what really is the purpose of this wealth that we have?

The true and ultimate purpose of wealth is the facilitation of relationships (follow me closely now).

First, let's all agree that "you can't take it with you" when you die, right? A few years ago, I heard about a man who desperately wanted to take his money with him when he died. In fact, he was so determined that when he was on his deathbed he said to his wife, "I want you to put all of my money in a chest in the attic, and when I die I'm going to grab it on the way up to Heaven." So she honored his request. Well, the man died not long after that, and, following the funeral, the woman went up to the attic to see if the money was still there—to see if he had actually grabbed it on the way up. Opening the chest, she found it still full of money. So she thought, "Maybe I should have put it in the basement!" Yes, it's true—you can't take it with you. Or, as I once heard Billy Graham say, "You'll never see a hearse pulling a U-Haul trailer." So that means that what you have when you die isn't really going to matter in an ultimate sense.

Second, let's all agree that relationships are the most meaningful things that we'll ever have in this life (and in the next, for that matter). Adrian Rogers often said, "If you want to know how rich you are, then add up everything that money can't buy and death can't take away—and then you'll know how rich you are." The answer to that little riddle is "relationships."

I credit my mother with the contents of this section, not least because one of her cardinal mantras has always been "people are more important than money," and she has always felt that spending money in order to build relationships is more important than stockpiling money beyond necessity. Now, she's a financially-responsible woman who's pretty conservative with her money—she's neither a spendthrift nor an ascetic. But she's always had the insight and wisdom to know that relationships with children, family, and friends are more important than money for the sake of money. Whereas my dad always had an excuse for why we couldn't do something as a family because of money, my mother always seemed to come up with a little bit of money for building relationships, experiences, and memories. She understood—and still understands to this day—the true purpose for wealth.

Ultimately, when it comes to the true purpose of riches, the question is: do you want to live rich or do you want to die rich? Yes, there are plenty of people who are dying rich these days. But have they *lived* rich? Are they rich in what really matters?

And, more important, are we?

Some Principles for Using Money

We've talked about some broad perspectives on money, and, hopefully, we've all gotten a little more clarity on wealth after reviewing those fundamentals. Now, let's talk about some specific and very practical principles that will make a difference in our lives when it comes to using the money that we have. Much of this information will not be new. But revisiting these principles is essential to maintaining (if not establishing in the first place) a financial equilibrium in our lives that will make for greater happiness, peace, and contentment.

Planning

Some men today are doing well with their money, but others are not. Some men have money left over at the end of the month while others seem to always have more month than money. Some men take well-aimed shots every time they pull the spending trigger while others shoot randomly from the hip—they just "spray and pray." Why? What makes the difference?

A financial plan makes all the difference in the world!

First and foremost, every man must have a budget. I know, I know, a lot of men don't like the "B" word, mostly because they see it as restrictive—kind of like a financial straitjacket. But, as financial guru Dave Ramsey often says, there are other "B" words that are worse than the word budget. How about *broke*? How about *bad* checks? How about *bankruptcy*?[4] Yes, there are definitely a lot of things worse than having a budget!

So where do you start? What's your plan?

In a recent article, Dave Ramsey offered some general guidelines for coming up with a sensible budget: "We recommend 10–15% for food, 25–35% on housing, 10–15% in savings, and 10–15% on charitable giving. And make sure your entire monthly budget— including clothing, transportation, insurance and entertainment— equals 100%."[5] In addition, Ramsey frequently shares his "Seven

Baby Steps" for getting your finances in order and on track. Here's the plan:

1. Step One. Set up a $1,000 emergency fund in the bank.
2. Step Two. Use the "debt snowball" to become debt free. List all of your debts (except your mortgage debt), from smallest to largest and put every extra dollar you can toward paying them off—from smallest to largest—while continuing to pay the minimum on the others. Move down the list until all debts are paid off.
3. Step Three. Set up a fully-funded emergency fund of three to six months of expenses.
4. Step Four. Begin investing 15% of your income.
5. Step Five. Begin saving for your children's college.
6. Step Six. Pay off your house.
7. Step Seven. Build wealth and give to others as much as you can.[6]

Ramsey's plan is certainly a life-long plan, since it will take most of us the better part of our lives to accomplish all the tasks on the list. But does his plan work? According to Ramsey, over 1,000,000 families since 1994 have used his plan to take ownership of their stuff—instead of being owned by their stuff. He claims that, by using this plan, the average family pays off $5,300 in debt and saves $2,700 in the first 90 days. I've known a number of men over the years who have gotten their financial affairs in order through Ramsey's plan, and I would highly recommend for men everywhere to get a copy of his book *Total Money Makeover.*[7]

The key to planning is to make a plan and then to actually execute the plan. Remember, *intentions* don't determine your destiny—*decisions* determine your destiny!

Waiting

So what's the greatest financial discipline that a man can have? Patience. And what's the number-one reason why so many men find themselves in dire straits? It's the "gotta-have-it-and-gotta-have-it-NOW" delusion. Ron Blue has put it this way:

Delayed gratification is the key to financial maturity; unless you spend less than you earn, no amount of income will be enough; that's why some people receive salary increases and soon find themselves even deeper in debt.[8]

While there's nothing wrong with debt as a tool for building your own prosperity—and that's exactly the *right* purpose for going in debt in the first place—there's everything wrong with debt when it's used to buy things you don't need with money that you don't have to impress people you don't even like. Or, as one man has said, "Debt provides us with the ability to pretend." And James MacDonald has said, "We've always talked about the two classes of the 'haves' and the 'have-nots.' Now we need to add a third category: the 'have-not-yet-paid-for-what-they-have' class!"[9]

In the recent past, one of the key contributing factors to this mountain of debt has been an alarming number of young married couples who try to have in 3 years what it took their parents 30 years to accumulate. Did you know, for instance, that in the average American home there are more televisions than people?! Yet we still wonder how the crazy train of debt and bankruptcy has gone off the rails.

At the end of the day, the desire for instant gratification will be the death of us financially—and emotionally, too. A recent article entitled "Debt-Induced Stress Continues for Many Americans" said, "About 46 percent of those surveyed say they're suffering from debt-related stress, with half of those people describing their stress as 'tremendous' or 'significant.'" This shouldn't surprise us, as the article points out that people today carry "an average of $44,000 in consumer debt through credit cards, auto loans, and other debt. This is a far bigger load than in the early 1980s, when per capita debt totaled about $14,000 in today's dollars."[10] That's 300 percent more debt per person! No wonder people are stressed out.

A few generations ago, only a few had been bitten by the "get-rich-quick" bug and the "gotta-have-it-now" bug. Times were simpler, and most people wouldn't think of living beyond their means. Patrick Morley, in his book *The Man in the Mirror*, recalls those days gone by:

> *The 1950s presented a picture of an ideal life. Yes, there were problems, but they were Chevrolet problems for Chevrolet families who lived in Chevrolet neighborhoods and had Chevrolet paychecks. Life was gradual; life was linear: Chevy, Buick, Oldsmobile, Cadillac, gold watch, funeral. The desire for instant gratification, however, has taken the place of [waiting for] a time when we can pay cash for our wants. For the last 40 years, on the other hand, the dominant economic theory in America has been consumerism—that a progressively greater consumption of goods is beneficial.*[11]

Nobody likes to wait on wealth—not me, not anybody. Everybody wants it to instantly fall into their lap. "If I could only hit the lotto," we often hear people say. Well, believe it or not, the lives of lottery winners (and others who get rich quick) oftentimes get worse—not better—after they "hit it big." Did you hear, for example, about Evelyn Adams? She won the New Jersey lottery not one but *two* times. So what happened to her $5.4 million in winnings? It's all gone, and now she lives in a trailer park. (I guess money really does talk—it says "good-bye!") Where did it go? Following her lotto wins, she became a compulsive gambler and also allowed family and friends to suck her dry with endless requests for money and favors. And then there's William Post. He won $16.2 million in the Pennsylvania lottery. But after blowing through his winnings, he now lives on $450 a month in Social Security and food stamps. On top of that, his ex-girlfriend sued him, he spent some time in jail for shooting over the head of a bill collector, and—of all things—his brother hired a hit man to kill him in hopes of inheriting some of William's wealth![12]

Sounds like a lot of those who get rich quick are likely candidates for the Jerry Springer show.

And what about all of these professional athletes who have blown their fortunes? These overpaid goons absolutely boggle our minds, don't they? How about these examples:

- Evander Holyfield is flat broke, even though he made $250 million in his career. But he squandered it buying a $20 million home with over 54,000 square feet, 109 rooms, a movie theatre, bowling alley, and Olympic-size pool—all on 235 acres of property.
- John Daly is also broke. He gambled away $60 million in career earnings. He once lost $1.65 million in five hours of playing the slot machines. On another occasion, he blew $1.2 million in two hours at a casino in Vegas.
- Mike Tyson, the king of blowing his money, squandered $400 million. On what? Well, he bought a $500,000 Bentley Continental (only 73 were ever made), another $4.5 million on other cars, a $2 million bathtub—not to mention $140,000 for two Bengal tigers. What an idiot! (By the way, I have no idea how much he paid for that ridiculous tattoo on his face.)[13]

Now, none of us will ever be in a position to blow millions of dollars. But we should be aware of the "gotta-have-it-and-gotta-have-it-now" delusion that instant credit brings. Above all things, it keeps us from being content with what we have. And isn't that really what it's all about—that is, being happy and at peace with what we have, realizing that the word "enough" is probably not a bad word? John Bogle tells this story in his book *Enough*:

> *At a party given by a billionaire, Kurt Vonnegut informed his pal, Joseph Heller, that their host, a very successful hedge fund manager, had made more money in a single day than Heller had earned from his wildly popular novel Catch 22 over its whole history. Heller responded, "Yes, but I have something that he will never have. I have enough."*[14]

So what's the way ahead on this issue of waiting? It's probably a good idea to buy absolutely nothing with credit short of a house and a car. I personally don't use credit to buy anything except a house and a car. A reasonable idea is to switch from credit cards to debit cards, with which money can only be spent if you actually have it in bank. Moreover, if you're married, agree with your wife to buy only what you can pay for with cash or a debit-card equivalent. If you do, then you'll be well on your way towards financial peace, freedom, and success.

Saving and Investing

So, what if you've found yourself under a mountain of debt and need to climb out from under it? Or what if you just need to accumulate some cash the old fashioned way? What do you do? You look back into the archives of solid financial wisdom, and you begin to save. It's a dated concept, I know. But the sound financial wisdom of setting aside something on a consistent basis has always paid huge dividends for those who choose to save.

So what about you—do you save anything every month? It doesn't have to be a lot, but it needs to be something. Unfortunately, fewer and fewer people have the foresight to save. In 1984, the average savings rate was 10.8%. That means that the average American put aside almost 11% of every paycheck. In 1994, that rate dropped to 4.8%, and in 2002 it had fallen to 1.8%. Then, in 2005, for the first time in our country's history, the rate dipped down to –0.5%, which means that the average American is now spending more than they make. About 40% of Americans say they are presently saving nothing for retirement. And one in four [25%] Americans told the Employee Benefit Research Institute that they have no savings at all.[15]

We can all learn a lesson from the "Baby Boomer" generation, the bulk of whom are retiring now. Have they set themselves up for success by saving over the years? Some have; many have not. In fact, the number of people nearing retirement these days who have "little or nothing" saved is staggering.

Saving has become a lost art, mostly because people would rather spend their money in the "now" instead of looking a little farther down the road and making decisions with the future in mind.

"Where and how do I start?" The most over-looked principle in saving is that people too often set up their standard of *living* before they set up their standard of *saving*. In other words, they live however they want (usually without a budget), and then they put whatever is left over into savings—if there *is* anything left over. Wouldn't it be better to decide what you're going to save each month before racking up bills and spending on other items? For example, you say at the beginning of each month, "I'm going to put 10% of my income in a savings account or other long-term investment then I'll live off the rest." Once you make a habit of putting aside a certain amount before ever spending anything each month, you'll be well on your way to having something substantial. Better yet, set up a direct deposit from your paycheck to a savings account or other investment so that you never even see that money—it just automatically goes into savings.

And what is the saving-and-investing potential? The truth may surprise you. For example, if, at the age of 25, you save $100.00 each month and invest it in a decent growth-style mutual fund or other investment, you could have $1.176 million in 40 years. And that's just one example. Financial expert Kimberly Palmer notes that if you were to save and invest $12,000 each year beginning at age 25, you'd have $3.2 million at age 65 (versus only $915,000 at age 65 if you started saving and investing that same $12,000 annually at age 40).[16]

But where should you put your savings? The stock market? What about real estate? What about a certificate of deposit or an IRA? Here are just a few ideas:

- <u>Total market fund</u>. Yes, the market got hammered not long ago. But the long-term picture is still very positive. And that's the perspective that any investor under 50 years of age should have—saving and investing for the long haul. What is a total market fund? It's a mutual fund that contains stocks from across the market. That way, you invest in the fund rather than betting on one or two stocks. Then, as the market goes, so goes your fund. And while the market may fluctuate temporarily at times, it will ultimately grow—and so will your money. Check out the Vanguard Group, as an example, for several different total market fund options (www.vanguard.com).

- <u>Roth IRA</u>. Unlike most other investment options, a Roth IRA allows you to pay no taxes on any interest that you earn. The trade off is that there are a few restrictions. First, you cannot draw any money out of it until your late 50s and early 60s without paying a nominal penalty—thus, making it a long-term investment for sure! Second, there is a limit to how much you can put into your Roth IRA each year. Currently, its $5,500 per individual or $11,000 per couple, so there's plenty of room for however much you want to invest (assuming that few men who read this book will have the wonderful problem of maxing out a Roth IRA each year with a ton of money left over). Operationally, Roth IRA funds are very much like mutual funds. Again, as a suggestion, check out the Vanguard Group to see what's out there.

- <u>Home ownership</u>. Money managers and investment counselors all agree on at least one thing: home ownership is probably the best investment that anyone can make over the course of their lifetime. Like the stock market, the real estate market has taken its licks over the years. But when compared to the average loss in stock and portfolio value, which for example was 30-35% across the board in the 2008 downturn, the value of most homes did not drop more than about 15-20%. For those with anything left over after maxing out a Roth IRA, buying a rental property is a good bet—provided that you have a trustworthy manager to oversee things for you or, better yet, you manage it yourself.

These are just a few options for putting your money to work, and it's impossible to say everything about saving and investing in a few paragraphs. But hopefully I've been able to raise your interest in how you can set yourself up for future success with whatever you have.

Sharing

There's one other financial discipline that we often overlook, and it's the discipline of sharing—that is, giving from our own resources to someone else. And it might sound strange that I'm even bringing it up, given the state of many people's finances as outlined above in various statistics. But, in addition to the obvious benefit that sharing has for the less fortunate or for the charitable organization to which you give, sharing has an incredible benefit for the giver, too.

Primarily, sharing keeps our own personal greed in check. Have you ever noticed how tightly we often hold on to our money? Most of us won't give it up for anything in the world. It reminds me of a time years ago when I was visiting some relatives. At the time, my younger cousin was about 5 years old. He was eating a bag of potato chips, and his mother said, "Thomas, why don't you share some of your chips with your cousin?" Thomas cried out, "No, no, no! Mine, mine, mine!" And then he ran out of the room.

Does that sound familiar?

While we may not act out in such an explicit way, we often struggle with greed nevertheless. It's the image of a fist clenched tightly around what belongs to us.

Here's a little exercise that you can do. Make a fist with your right hand and squeeze it as hard as you can. Hold it, hold it, squeeze tighter, hold it, hold it, squeeze tighter, hold it . . . OK, now release. You see? Squeezing so tightly for so long represents what our greed does to our bodies, hearts, and minds. But the act of giving—really, of releasing our grip on our money and our stuff—relieves us of that tension. Of course, we don't have to give all of our stuff away, but there probably ought to be a little something that we set aside on a regular basis to share with others. They need it, but the truth is that we often need to give it more than they need to receive it.

Think about this phenomenon in nature. In the Middle East, there is a body of water called "the Dead Sea." And why is it called that? Technically, the amount of salt in the water is too high to sustain life. But there's also a secondary reason: the Dead Sea takes in water from rain, runoff, and river flow, but it gives absolutely nothing in return— no life, no water, no nothing. It always takes, but it never gives.

Just like saving, sharing and giving is a discipline that will fall by the wayside if we don't have a strategy. As with saving, most people establish their standard of living before they set a standard for giving. So, for starters, why not carve out 5 percent of your income at the beginning of the month and find a worthy cause for it? Maybe your church, maybe a local charity, or maybe someone you personally know who needs it more than you do. You'll be blessed in more than a few ways if you establish the habit of sharing as a principle in your home.

Dave Ramsey featured a story on one of his videos about a family who was trying to pay off their debt so that they could adopt a child from overseas. They had a total of $60,000 in debt, and they had paid off all but $10,000 (they decided that they wouldn't adopt until after they'd paid off all of their debt). At the same time, they really wanted to buy a trampoline for their other kids. One day, they ran into a couple they recognized from church but didn't know personally. They were all taking a Dave Ramsey class at church, so when the other couple asked how the family was doing, they explained how they were paying off their debt, how they wanted to adopt, and how they wanted to buy a trampoline for their kids. It was a casual conversation that ended in just a few minutes. A few days later, a new trampoline showed up at the family's house—it was a gift from the couple they had casually spoken with earlier. Gratefully, they immediately set it up in their backyard and their kids went wild on it. A few more days went by, and the family received a call from the same couple saying, "You seem like nice people; we've got a deal for you." At that point, the family thought, "Uh oh, here comes some crazy sales pitch for something we don't need or want. They used the trampoline to get into our lives as part of the sales pitch." But the couple was persistent and came over to talk. Just when the family thought the couple was about to drop the sales "bomb," they actually said, "We want to pay off your remaining $10,000 in debt so that you can go ahead and adopt. Now, how do you spell your names so we can write you a check?" Dumbfounded, the family accepted a check for $10,000 right there on the front porch and was able to adopt a little baby girl soon thereafter. The couple's only condition was that the family wouldn't tell anyone what they had done.[17]

When you read that story, you might find yourself saying, "I wish someone would do that for me!" Or maybe . . . just maybe . . . you find yourself saying, "I want to be a position to do something like that for someone else." Well, if you get a handle on your money and possessions and put them to work for you rather than seeing it only as a means to get more, you may one day be able to bless others in a similar way.

Now's the Time

"My care of equipment shall set the example for others to follow." A more elite man will take that statement seriously.

This chapter is filled with good ideas. In fact, it probably has more practical ideas than any other part of the whole book. But the problem with good ideas is that we like to agree that they look good and appealing, but then we don't necessarily put them into practice.

Your care of your cash and possessions—your care of equipment—will impact your life one way or another. So make the most of the wealth that God has given you, whether talking about giving thanks for what you have, using it to build relationships, or watching it grow as you set it aside and put it to work over the long haul. Determine today to choose wisely. Remember, your decisions determine your destiny!

6

Spiritual Athlete Warrior: Personal Training in God's Gym

RAW—Ranger Athlete Warrior. All Rangers know about the RAW program, a fitness training strategy designed to take Rangers beyond the basics of push-ups, sit-ups, and the two-mile run. The stated purpose of RAW is "to provide education and training that optimize the physical/mental development and sustainment of the Ranger's most lethal weapon—the Ranger himself."[1] The goals are comprehensive: achieve a level of physical fitness equal to that required of a Ranger combat mission, understand and apply sound nutritional practices, develop mental toughness, and receive training in injury prevention and treatment. Ultimately, RAW is designed to better prepare Rangers for the physical and mental rigors of sustained ground combat. With an emphasis upon the numerous athletic skills required of a complete warrior, it's an effective program that brings Rangers to a higher level of overall physical fitness and readiness for war.

But a more elite man also faces a spiritual and emotional battle every day of his life. He faces battles with temptation from sin, authenticity with his family, balance between his vocation and meaningful relationships, and isolation from other men of wisdom and faith. What about the *spiritual* fitness required for those battles? After all, God has created us as physical, emotional, and spiritual beings—body, soul, and spirit—and we've got fire on "all three cylinders" if we're going to energetically fight the daily battles of life. To do that, I want to introduce the SAW program—Spiritual Athlete Warrior.

Go to the Spiritual Gym!

In the ancient world, athletic competitions were a big deal—very much like our culture today. And Paul, one of the writers of the New Testament, was a huge sports fan. In fact, he often drew analogies between the sporting events of his day and the spiritual truths he sought to communicate. For example:

We wrestle not against flesh and blood but against the rulers, authorities, and cosmic powers over this present darkness, against the spiritual forces of evil in the heavenly places. (Ephesians 6:12)

Those who run in a race all run, but only one receives the prize. So, run in such a way that you might win. Everyone who competes in the games exercises self-discipline in all things. They compete to receive a crown made of earthly things, but we run to receive a heavenly crown—a crown that lasts forever. Therefore, I do not run in vain; I do not box as one who is merely beating the air. Rather, I discipline my body and make it my slave. (1 Corinthians 9:24-27)

Train yourselves to be godly. For physical exercise has some value, but godliness has value for all things, holding promise both for this present life and the life to come. (1 Timothy 4:7-8)

In the last passage, Paul used the language of the physical training facility. In fact, the Greek word that translates into the word "train" is the word *gumnadzo* (Paul wrote his letters in the Greek language of his day), which is closely related to the Greek term *gumnasium*—the word from which we get our words "gymnasium" and "gym." So when Paul said, "Train yourselves to be godly," he basically said, "Go to the spiritual gym!" In Ranger language, Paul is talking about SAW—the Spiritual Athlete Warrior program.

What is SAW? It's basically a daily, disciplined walk with God by which we increase our devotion to him, our knowledge about him, and our influence for him. SAW doesn't have an ultimate endstate here on earth; rather, it's a lifelong pursuit of godliness that never really ends until we get to heaven. But the desired daily goal is that we are more able to energetically meet our enemies in the spiritual warfare of this life.

And what are the benefits of the SAW program? In many ways, they spiritually mirror those of the RAW program but go far beyond even those benefits. Or as Paul said, spiritual fitness (that is, "godliness") has benefits both for this life and for the life to come.

Of course, in many ways, this entire book has highlighted the benefits of godliness for earthly life here and now. And as Paul mentioned, those benefits stretch into eternity, not least because they set us up for success in the life to come, eternal life. When you think about it, there's absolutely no reason to neglect the SAW program when you consider all that it does here and hereafter.

SAW: In It to Win It

If there's one phrase that completely describes Rangers, it's that they're "in it to win it"—whatever "it" may be. For sure, there's a determination in the heart of every Ranger to succeed at whatever he does. And when it comes to physical fitness, Rangers truly go above and beyond. Whether it's RAW, Gym Jones, Cross Fit, or any number of other advanced workout programs, you will see Rangers doing it. These guys are relentless!

Going back to one of Paul's athletic passages, we see him comparing the dogged determination of the professional athletes of his day with a passionate pursuit of godliness and spiritual fitness:

Those who run in a race all run, but only one receives the prize. So, run in such a way that you might win. Everyone who competes in the games exercises self-discipline in all things. They compete to receive a crown made of earthly things, but we run to receive a heavenly crown—a crown that lasts forever. Therefore, I do not run in vain; I do not box as one who is merely beating the air. Rather, I discipline my body and make it my slave. (1 Corinthians 9:24-27)

Paul uses athletic imagery here from the Olympic games of his day to illustrate a key point: the SAW program is not for cowards or spiritual marshmallows! Rather, attaining a deep level of godliness takes determination, self-discipline, and good old-fashioned W-O-R-K.

Of course, more than anyone else, Rangers can appreciate the hard work that a physically-strong body requires. But what about this idea that spiritual fitness likewise takes a serious investment of time and energy? If we're to believe what Paul had to say, then we must all agree that the SAW program is no joke.

But at the same time, as Paul also said, it has much value for this life and for the life to come. On an earthly level, the SAW program enhances everything that makes life worth living—things like peace, righteousness, and legacy. Believe it: life is just better when God is at the center. Of course, let's not forget that there are eternal rewards for those who participate in SAW, because those who do so receive a "heavenly crown." And what could be better than that?

So, are you in it to win it?

SAW: The Disciplines

OK, it's time to get down to business. It's time to talk about the actual exercises and disciplines that go into the SAW program. This is, as they say, where the rubber meets the road.

I think what I like best about the SAW program is that it's a strategy—a clear plan—that can be followed by anyone. And we all know the value of having a structured strategy rather than a will-of-the-wisp approach to working out in the gym, right? I mean, we've all seen the guy in the gym who comes in, does a few reps on the bench, maybe does a few curls with the women's dumbbells, gets on the treadmill for a few minutes, and then leaves. There's no plan to his workout, and, of course, that guy doesn't get anything out of it.

How much better to have a plan—say, chest and triceps on one day, back and biceps on the next day, shoulders on the next day, legs the next day, and then start over again? Yes, the guy who brings his little notebook with him to the gym, marks down his reps and weight, and abides by his pre-determined workout plan is the guy who will always keep himself physically strong.

It's really the same with spiritual fitness. You can't expect to be a Spiritual Athlete Warrior if you just occasionally read a verse or two from the Bible, pray just every now and again, and attend church only when you've got nothing else to do on Sunday. Rather, you've got to have a plan and you've got to follow that plan.

That's where the disciplines of the SAW program come into play. They give us a plan that can be executed on a regular basis. Here's a list of the disciplines that we'll cover in this chapter:

1. Studying
2. Praying
3. Gathering

4. Serving
5. Influencing

Let's take a few minutes and talk about each of these, both in terms of what they are and also how we can incorporate them consistently in to our lives.

STUDYING: The Bread of Life

There I was, lying in a shallow fighting position (a "Ranger grave") on day 8 of the Florida phase of Ranger School. The last 50 days had taken their toll on my 32-year-old body, not least because we had been on limited rations throughout the experience. As I laid there in that patrol base perimeter looking for the "enemy," I began thinking about all of the things that I wanted to eat. Then, I looked down on the rim of that little hole and saw an ant crawling by. But this wasn't any ordinary ant; it was an ant with a small cracker crumb in his mouth. He was probably carrying it back to his hole for a meal. And for about 20 seconds, I watched this ant crawl by and thought to myself, "I'll bet I could wrestle that cracker away from that ant and have myself something to eat!" But, sadly, in my weakened condition I didn't have the strength even to beat an ant!

Everybody has an "I-was-starving" story from Ranger School, and I'm no exception. Yes, if Ranger School teaches us anything, it teaches us the importance of eating something decent before attempting anything physically demanding.

And so it is with spiritual fitness and the SAW program. You see, there's such a thing as spiritual sports nutrition, and it begins and ends with something called "the Bread of Life."

Throughout the Bible, the words of God are compared to food, and all of God's people are encouraged to partake of that food. Think about some of these passages:

The Lord your God led you all the way in the desert for forty years. He humbled you, causing you to hunger and then feeding you with manna, to teach you that man does not live on bread alone but on every word that comes from the mouth of the Lord. (Deuteronomy 8:2-3)

The people said to Jesus, "Our forefathers ate the manna in the desert; as it is written, 'He gave them bread from heaven to eat.'" And Jesus said to them, I tell you the truth; it is not Moses who has given you the bread from heaven, but it is my Father who gives you the true bread from heaven. For the bread of God is he who comes down from heaven and gives life to the world . . . I am the bread of life. He who comes to me will never go hungry." (John 6:31-35)

So how does a man partake of this bread? By studying, believing, and applying the word of God, the Bible, to his life, that's how. So let's talk about practical ways to do that.

First, there is **the personal study of the Bible**, and this happens when we sit down, open a Bible, and actually *read* it. Sounds easy enough, right? Yet, as we all know, it's easier to talk about it than to do it. Let me give you some ideas for beefing up your private time eating this bread:

- Read a chapter from the book of Proverbs every day. There are 31 chapters in the book and generally there are 30 days in a month. If today is the 15th, then read Proverbs 15; if today is the 24th, read Proverbs 24—you get the idea, right? You could have the entire book read in a month. Along the way, you're going to find out that Proverbs is one of the easiest books in the Bible to understand because it's so very relevant to our lives. Even though it was written thousands of years ago, it makes perfect sense today. In fact, if you read Proverbs for two or three months in a row, you're going to find that, throughout the day, your mind goes back to what you've read time and again because of how well it relates to life in the twenty-first century. It's too easy!

- Read a psalm from the book of Psalms each day. There are 150 psalms in the Bible, so it will take you a little longer than a month to do it, but the results will be fantastic. Whereas Proverbs deals with daily life, the psalms often deal with praising God, deeper devotion to God, or the anguish that life's difficulties bring. Reading the psalms is a great exercise for strengthening your emotional and spiritual cardiovascular system.
- Choose a specific book from the Bible and start to read it, maybe a few chapters each day. The books that are based on interesting stories—like Joshua, 1 & 2 Samuel, Nehemiah, and the Gospel of John are great places to start. (The first book of the Bible I ever read "from cover to cover" was Joshua—it's a great story.)
- Get a devotional booklet like "Our Daily Bread." These kinds of booklets list a couple of short Bible passages to read for the day, maybe a couple of additional passages that are part of a "read-your-Bible-through-in-a-year" program, along with some devotional thoughts on what you've just read. The notes for reading your Bible cover-to-cover in one year are great, and keeping up with that agenda throughout the year will definitely keep you in your Bible.
- Begin a habit of memorizing verses from the Bible. "I have hidden your word in my heart, that I might not sin against you" (Psalm 119:11) are the words of a man seriously committed to walking with God. Indeed, you will be amazed at the spiritual power which comes from being able

to recall throughout the day verses from the Bible that you've committed to memory. Where to start? Here's a "Top Ten" list you can try out:

- **Psalm 34:1** – "I will bless the Lord at all times; his praise will always be on my lips."
- **John 3:16** – "For God so loved the world that he gave his one and only son, that whosoever believes in him will not perish but will have everlasting life."
- **Philippians 4:13** – "I can do all things through Christ who strengthens me."
- **Proverbs 3:5-6** – "Trust in the Lord and lean not on your own understanding; in all you ways acknowledge him, and he will direct your paths.
- **Psalm 20:7** – "Some trust in horses and some trust in chariots, but we will remember the name of the Lord our God."
- **Psalm 63:1** – "God, you are my God; earnestly I seek you. My soul longs for you; my body thirsts for you, in a dry and weary land where there is no water."
- **Psalm 73:25-26** – "Who do I have in heaven, but you? And on earth, there is nothing I desire besides you. My heart and my flesh may fail, but God is the strength of my heart and my portion forever."
- **1 Peter 5:6** – "Humble yourself under God's mighty hand, and he will lift you up in due time."
- **John 3:27** – "A man can receive nothing unless it has been given to him from heaven."
- **Ephesians 2:8-10** – "For it is by grace you have been saved, through faith—and this not of yourselves, it is the gift of God—not by works, so that no one can

boast. For we are God's workmanship, created in Christ Jesus to do good works."

- Most of us spend a lot of time listening to music in our cars or while working out. Why not spend some of that time listening to some great teaching from the Word? Get the podcasts of an exciting, dynamic Bible teacher and listen to them on a regular basis. These are essentially sermons that these guys have delivered and then posted on the internet for free downloading. Don't know where to start? I would highly recommend checking out James MacDonald (www.walkintheword.com) or my own website (www.philkramer.org). If you really want to dive deep, try Ravi Zacharias (www.rzim.org).

- Get some books from a Christian bookstore and *read them*. There are all sorts of books out there that deal with just about every topic you can imagine. There are books that talk about being a better man, about being a better husband, about getting ready to be a husband, about theology, about history, about warfare and combat, about hunting—all from a biblical perceptive. So even though you aren't reading the Bible, per se, you're nevertheless engaging with biblical truths as you read these books. (The book you're holding in your hands right now is just one of many examples.)

If you get on board with this spiritual workout schedule I've listed above and follow it consistently, you'll be amazed at how "big" you get in a short time. It's like taking spiritual steroids!

Second, there is **the public study of the Bible**, and this happens when we gather with other people to study the Bible. This can take place in a large-group setting (like going to a solid, dynamic, Bible-teaching church) or in a small-group setting (some people call this "Bible study," some people might call it "Sunday School," and still others might simply call it a "small group"). Of course, getting involved in public Bible study takes a little more effort than personal Bible study, if only because you actually have to get up and go find a group of people to study the Bible with. But when you do, you will grow by leaps and bounds.

By the way, be sure to get your own copy of the Bible and bring it whenever you go someplace to study the Bible publicly. Research shows that we remember 30 percent of what we hear, but we remember 70 percent of what we see. And it definitely makes a difference to have a Bible in your hands when you're studying it—right? And while you're at it, don't forget to bring something to write with (every good Ranger always has something to write with!) and something to write on. Why? So you can take notes of what is said. Again, if you're actively engaging with the lesson to the point that you're writing some of it down, you're much more likely to retain and learn something. Or as someone has said, "The dullest pencil is still better than the sharpest mind."

So here are some things to think about when getting involved in a group:

- When looking for a **large-group** setting (like a church service), look for one that takes the Bible seriously. And how do you know if they take the Bible seriously? Examine how the teacher interacts with the Bible. If he reads a passage from the Bible and then doesn't really interact with that passage for the rest of his message, that's a big red flag. On the other hand, the ideal is where the teacher reads the passage and then interacts with it throughout his message. Some people call this "expository" teaching, which basically means that the teacher basically gives a verse-by-verse explanation of what the Bible says in the passage. This is, without question, the ideal kind of public teaching.

- Another thing to think about when attending a **large-group** Bible study is the way that the teacher challenges you to do something great as a response to studying the Bible. After all, there are a lot of Bible teachers who look good and sound good, but who don't really lay any challenge at our feet. For example, there's a story about Abraham Lincoln going to church with his assistant. After the service, his assistant said, "What did you think about the sermon? Did you think the preacher was successful?" And Lincoln said, "He was very eloquent, very learned, and very persuasive. But I do not believe he succeeded." Puzzled, the assistant asked, "But why not?" Lincoln answered, "Because he did not challenge us to do something great." Hmmm. So examine the teaching that you're getting on a regular basis and ask, "Am I being challenged to do something great—to raise the bar in my life in a significant way?" If not, then you probably should go someplace where you get that kind of challenge.

- When attending a **small-group** study, make sure that you bring something with you when you attend. And what do I mean by that? I'm not talking about bringing a Bible—we've already talked about that. Rather, I'm talking about prayerful preparation and earnest expectation. In other words, spend some time in prayer before showing up and specifically ask God to speak to you and fulfill your spiritual hunger in the class. Likewise, show up expecting to get something significant out of the lesson.

- Now, when you're attending a **small-group** study, think about the whole reason why you're going to that group. After all, you're there because it's more personal than a 300, 500, or 1,000-person church service. But what happens in most small-group settings? Only a very few people in the group actually interact, while everyone else just sits there taking up real estate and oxygen. So, if you're seriously going to get something out of these small-group Bible studies, then get engaged: ask questions, make observations, and talk about how the material is becoming a part of your life. Ask anyone who's spent a significant amount of time in college and graduate studies, and they'll tell you that people learn best when they get engaged with the material and the teacher.

You see, there are many practical ways and places to get a hold of this bread. So ask yourself, "Am I really hungry for spiritual food?" If so, then go out and get some!

PRAYER: Talking with the Father

"Prayer is like air. And just as we can't live physically without breathing, we can't survive spiritually without praying."

Those words are true, and most people of faith would acknowledge the power and importance of prayer. And everyone would also acknowledge that praying daily is ideal. But talking about it and doing it are two totally different things, right?

How many of you have ever tried to pray, only to have your prayer go something like this: "Lord, thank you for this day and thank you for all of the many blessings that you've give me. Thank you for my family, my job, and . . . zzzzzzzzzz." Or what about the inevitable distractions that enter our minds as we pray? You begin to pray, and you find yourself, for example, praying for your parents. You begin to thank God for their health. But then your mind starts wandering, and you remember a baseball game that you attended with your dad last year. And then you remember getting ketchup on your clothes from the huge hotdog you were eating. And then you remember that you need to do laundry. Now, how in the world did you get from praying for your parents to doing the laundry?!

As much as any other part of the SAW program, you've got

to have a plan for your prayer time, otherwise you'll end up either wandering around in your mind or you'll fall asleep. Fortunately, there are some practical ideas that will help you make the most of your time in God's gym.

And let's not forget that prayer is basically a conversation with your Father in heaven. Isn't that what we're talking about when we talk about prayer—time with the Father? Yes, just like Jesus said:

When you pray, go into your room, close the door, and pray to your Father, who is unseen. (Matthew 6:6)

Yes, prayer is basically a conversation with our Father who is in heaven. It doesn't have to involve flowery language: "Thou art worthy, and I prayest to Thee for all yonder people who sufferest from manifold maladies." Rather, prayer happens when you open your heart to God and talk to him honestly and openly.

When describing prayer in those terms, it sounds great! But oftentimes when people try to pray without a plan, they hit on a few items and then, because they can't think of anything else off the top of their heads, they quit praying. And that's why having a plan is vitally important—and actually, it's pretty easy.

A-C-T-S: A Practical Plan for Praying

Shortly after I became a Christian, I went to a summer youth camp in Orlando, Florida. While there, a guy gave a class on having an organized prayer time, and he used the acronym A-C-T-S to give us some structure for our praying. It's a very simply plan that I've used now for over 20 years.

First, **"A" stands for "adoration."** You start your prayer time by worshipping God—basically, by telling him how great he is and how worthy he is of praise and worship. It's really a great way to start your prayer time, because it puts everything in perspective and frames the rest of what you will later say in prayer.

By the way, it's important to note that worship, adoration, and praise are responses to who God is, not necessarily to what he has done or our perception of what he has done. (Responding to what God has done is called "thanksgiving," and we'll cover that in a minute.) This is important to note, because God deserves our adoration at all times and not just when he think he's done something positive for us or our families. Sometimes we hear people say, "God is good, all the time; and all the time, God is good!" But typically we only hear people say that when something good has happened in their lives such as getting a promotion at work or their sick child gets well. But what if they lose their job or their child doesn't recover? Is God still good? Does he still deserve adoration and praise? In short, "yes" he deserves all of that because his worthiness is not contingent upon what he does for us. It hangs entirely upon who he is. That's why David in the Bible could say, "I will bless the Lord at all times, his praise will always be on my lips" (Psalm 34:1).

Now, you might be thinking, "What do I say? How do I go about worshipping God?" Well, a great idea is to go straight to the Bible and "pray" some of the psalms or other passages that talk about God's greatness. (Yes, that's right: you can read from the Bible and use the words as part of your prayers.) For starters, try any of these out; but there are many, many more:

Psalm 8:1-9	Psalm 111:1-10	Isaiah 64:4
Psalm 19:1-14	Psalm 113:1-9	John 20:24-28
Psalm 29:1-11	Psalm 145:1-21	Romans 11:33-36
Psalm 47:1-9	Psalm 147:1-20	Philippians 2:5-11
Psalm 63:1-11	Psalm 148:1-14	Revelation 4:8-11
Psalm 66:1-20	Psalm 149:1-9	Revelation 5:11-14

Of course, you don't have to pray through all of these—just select one or two each time you sit down to pray. But I think you get the point: use the Scripture to help you know what to pray and how to pray. After all, many of these passages started out as prayers in somebody's heart, so use them as such in your own life, too.

Another good idea is to go to the hymns and songs of praise that the people of God have used over the years. While many churches have quit using hymnals, I have one at home. Sometimes I'll go to a page and read (or sometimes even sing!) the words of a song as part of my "adoration" of the Lord. How about these words, for example:

O Lord my God, when I in awesome wonder,
Consider all the works Thy hands have made;
I see the stars, I hear the rolling thunder,
Thy power throughout the universe displayed.

Then sings my soul, "My savior, God to Thee,"
"How great Thou art, how great Thou art;"
Then sings my soul, "My savior, God to Thee,"
"How great Thou art, how great Thou art!"[2]

Or how about a more "contemporary" song?

From the ends of the earth,
To the depths of the sea,
From the heights of the heavens,
Your name be praised!

From the hearts of the weak,
To the shouts of the strong,
From the lips of all people,
This song we raise, Lord!

Throughout the endless ages,
You will be crowned with praises,
Lord most high!
Exalted in every nation,
Sovereign of all creation,
Lord most! Be magnified![3]

Now, some of you guys might feel a little uncomfortable with the idea of worshipping God in private. It may not seem natural. If that's the case, then I want to ask you this question: how much of your life is filled with worshipping God—that is, are you setting the conditions so that worship is a natural part of your life? If not, then it's hardly surprising that the idea of worshipping privately seems odd. But if you're actively filling your life with worship, then worshipping privately in prayer will seem natural.

So what are some ways to more effectively fill your life with worship? One specific way is to consistently attend a dynamic church where worshipping God in song is highlighted as important and life-changing. This kind of church places a great emphasis on collective worship and deliberately encourages everyone to get engaged—men included! Yes, it's not enough simply to stand there and mumble a few of the words or simply observe others singing. You, the man, must get engaged in worship. And on a side note, there are few things that will leave a greater and more lasting impression on your children than for them to see you singing and engaging in musical worship at church.

Beyond that, another great way to fill your life with worship is to listen to God-honoring music throughout the week. Yes, there are other interesting things to listen to at work or while you're driving around, not least of which are various genres of non-Christian music, news, sports radio, or any number of political talk shows . . . and there's nothing wrong with any of that. But none of those other things will fill your life with worship and an abiding sense of the eternal. So

I would encourage you to spend more of your time listening to music that exalts God and reminds you of his place in your life.

On that note, one of the most measurable metrics for worship in your life is, "How often do worship songs come to your mind throughout the week?" In other words, as you work out in the gym, drive down the road, or walk down the hallway at work, how often does a song about God just pop into your head? If you're effectively filling your life with worship, it probably happens a good bit. If worshipping actively in church or listening to worship music at other times isn't a habit for you, then you're probably not hearing those songs in your mind at other times. For me, one result of filling my life with worship has been that oftentimes the very first thing that comes to mind when I wake up in the morning (perhaps even before I open my eyes) and the very last thing that crosses my mind before I drift off to sleep at night is a worship song I've recently heard. When that happens on a regular basis, I know that my life is being filled with worship. When it doesn't happen very often, I know that I need to be more deliberate about worship.

Why do I mention all this about filling your life with worship? It's because worshipping God with adoration is the best way to start your prayer time, but if your life is not filled with worship then getting engaged in your time of prayer is going to be very difficult and awkward. But if worship is a habit you've deliberately cultivated throughout the week, then you could easily spend 5-10 minutes of prayer time in adoration of God without even realizing where the time has gone. In fact, you'll be amazed how easy it is to tell God how much you love him and how much he means to you.

Second, **"C" stands for "confession."** After you've put all things into perspective of who God is, then you need to take a few minutes to humbly confess who you are in light of who God is. And that means that you need to sincerely confess to God how you've fallen short of his holiness and righteousness. It's called sin, and it's something that

I do every day and something that you do every day. But the good news is that we can confess our sins to God and receive forgiveness for every one of them:

> *If we confess our sins, he is faithful and just and will forgive us our sins and purify us from all unrighteousness.* (1 John 1:9)

This principle of confession is important, because if we're not being open and honest with God, then we can't have the kind daily relationship with him that he wants and that we want. I like how the Bible says that if we confess our sins, God will cover them up; but, on the other hand, if we try to cover them up, then God will keep them out in the open:

> *He who conceals his sin does not prosper, but whoever confesses and renounces them finds mercy.* (Proverbs 28:13)

Or think about how God says that he will not listen to our prayers if we try to hide sin in our hearts instead of confessing them to him:

> *I cried out to God with my mouth; his praise was on my tongue. If I had cherished sin in my heart, the Lord would not have listened.* (Psalm 66:17-18)

Again, you can incorporate Scripture into your prayers, such as this powerful confession of sin that David made after he got busted for having sex with Bathsheba:

> *Have mercy on me, O God, according to your unfailing love; according to your great compassion, blot out my transgressions. Wash away all my iniquity and cleanse me from my sin. For I know my transgressions, and my sin is always before me. Against*

you, you only have I sinned and done what is evil in your sight. Create in me a clean heart, O God, and renew a steadfast spirit within me. Restore to me the joy of your salvation and grant me a willing spirit to sustain me. (Psalm 51:1-4, 10-12)

Be sure that you take time to confess your sins individually rather than say in some gray and fuzzy way, "Lord, *if* I have sinned, forgive me." Hey, you know exactly what you've done in the last 24 hours, so check them off and get them forgiven. And I might also emphasize the importance of daily confession—that is, keep a short list with God. Also, after you've confessed those sins to God and received forgiveness, don't forget to thank him for forgiving yours sins.

Now, just as with adoration, confession is an awesome part of prayer that will lift your heart. And, if you follow some of the ideas given above, you'll have spent 5-10 minutes talking with God about confession and forgiveness without even knowing that the time has gone.

Third, **"T" stands for "thanksgiving."** This is where you get the privilege to take a few minutes and tell God how grateful you are for all that he has done and is doing in your life and in the lives of others. As we've already said, adoration is a response to who God is; thanksgiving in a response to what God has done. This is one of my favorite times in prayer, not least because it's so easy to think about things to be thankful for. And if John 3:27 (which we've already cited a few times in this book) is true—"a man can receive nothing unless it has been given to him from heaven"—then just about anything you can think of is something to be thankful for.

Once again, go to the Scripture for motivation, words, and ideas for giving thanks to God:

Shout for joy to the Lord, all the earth. Worship the Lord with gladness; come before him with joyful songs. Know that the Lord is God. It is he who made us, and we are his. We are his people, the sheep of his pasture. Enter his gates with thanksgiving and his courts with praise; give thanks to him and praise his name. For the Lord is good and his mercy endures forever; his faithfulness continues through all generations. (Psalm 100:1-5)

As I take time to give God thanks, here's just a sampling of the things I mention:

Jesus	Salvation	Health and Strength
Shara (my wife)	My children	My mother
My brother and his family	Fun memories with my family	My calling as a minister and chaplain
Rangers and their Families	Food, clothing, other material blessings	Money in the bank

The list literally goes on and on. I would guess that you could spend an entire hour just listing all of the things that you're thankful for. How sad it is when we don't take any time at all!

Fourth, **"S" stands for "supplication."** Of course, you're probably thinking, "What in the world is supplication?!" Well, that's just a fancy word that means "praying for other people and praying for yourself." Usually when we talk about prayer, this is what most people think about—and it's an important part of prayer. But it only comes after adoration, confession, and thanksgiving have set the stage for our supplication.

When I first became a Christian and learned this A-C-T-S approach to prayer, I got caught up in the mistaken idea that I had to pray for everybody and everything *every time* I sat down to pray. In fact, I took a sheet of paper and wrote down the names of just about everyone I knew and then, every day, tried to pray for every person on that entire list. Needless to say, it took a long time. To be honest, it got a little boring, too.

So, after a while of doing that and getting bogged-down on a regular basis, I got an idea. I divided the entire list by 7 and then assigned an equal number of people to each day of the week (though I still kept certain people and a few specific issues on the side so that I would pray for them every day). That way, I was praying through the whole list on a weekly basis, but I was also getting some variety each day so that I wasn't getting bogged-down on the same list—the same *long* list—every day. And to this day, it's still an important part of my time in prayer.

- First, I pray for my mother, brother, and his family
- Then I go down to that certain day of the week and pray for those under that day. I don't necessarily pray long prayers for each one, but I mention them generally and then specifically for any needs they might have presently. (By the way, it's a great idea to choose one person from that day's prayer list and send then an e-mail or text of encouragement letting them know that you're praying for them and asking them about their latest prayer needs. It's a great way to keep in touch with that person from one month to the next.)
- Lastly, I pray every day for a few significant items as well as my immediate family.

Just so you know what I'm talking about, let me lay out a sample prayer card that I put together. Of course, I'm just using fake names for this example prayer card (names of various celebrities—God knows they need some *serious* prayer!), but I think you get the idea:

Mother	**Friday**
Steve and Sarah	Pamela Anderson
	Dog the Bounty Hunter
Monday	Flavor Flav
Ozzy Osbourne	
Madonna	**Saturday**
Lady Ga Ga	Snoop Dog
	Hugh Heffner
Tuesday	Bruce Springsteen
Paris Hilton	
Axel Rose	**Sunday**
AC DC	Bret Michaels
	Eddie van Halen
Wednesday	David Lee Roth
Dennis Rodman	
Ellen Degeneres	
Rosie O'Donnell	Shara
	Emma Layne
Thursday	Libby
Britney Spears	Baur
Lindsey Lohan	Lightsey
Bill Clinton	Adrian

Remember, I put certain people on here that I pray for every day (my mother, my brother Steve and his wife Sarah) along with my immediate family (my wife and five children). And while I have three names assigned to each day on this example card, my actual card has about 6-7 names per day. When you think about it, this is a pretty efficient way of praying for many people without either (1) getting bogged down with a long list or (2) getting too redundant day after day after day.

Of course, this is just one technique among many. There are numerous other ways of getting the job done. But I've had a lot of success with the A-C-T-S approach, and I would guess that it might work for you, too.

GATHERING: God's Family of Friends

After studying and praying, the next most-important part of the SAW program is what I call "gathering." Basically, I'm talking about getting together with other people who have faith in Jesus. Some people call it "church," but gathering is much broader than merely going to a church service. And it's not so much the *what* or the *where* that makes the difference; it's the *who* and the *why* of gathering that's so powerful.

By the way, there are always going to be some folks who say something like, "Hey, I believe in God and Jesus and all of that, but I can worship God all by myself in the woods or on a bass boat or . . ." (implying, "I don't need church or any of that stuff"). And, yes, it's true that you can worship God in all of those places (and I hope you *are* worshipping God when you go to the woods or go fishing or whatever). But that doesn't mean that gathering with other believers in Jesus isn't important or necessary. In fact, I kind of wonder about those people who say, "I don't need to go to church" or "I don't believe in 'organized' religion." I like to ask them, "So what do you do with these verses?"

Jesus said, "Wherever two or more gather together in my name, there I am with them." (Matthew 18:20)

The body is a unit, though it is made up of many parts; and though all of its parts are many, they form one body. So it is with Christ. For we were all baptized by one Spirit into one body. (1 Corinthians 12:12)

You received the Spirit of adoption [so that] the Spirit himself testifies with our spirit that we are God's children. [And consider]

> *how great is the love that the Father has lavished on us, that we*
> *should be called children of God!* (Romans 8:15-16; 1 John 3:1)

> *Let us not neglect gathering together, as some are in the habit of*
> *doing, but let us [gather] to encourage one another—and all the*
> *more as you see the Day approaching.* (Hebrews 10:25)

Yes, I just threw a bunch of Bible verses at you that, on the surface, might not have much to do with one another. But think about the common theme that runs throughout all of them: *gathering.*

In the first passage, Jesus essentially said that he visits with those who *gather* in his name. In the second passage, we see that God uses the image of the human body to represent an organization or entity. This was actually a common illustration in the ancient world—for example, the Roman Empire was described as a "body." The point of the illustration is that we are all different, but we're all a part of a larger element. And the implication is that no single part of the body should be cut off from the rest—that is, we're meant to be *together.* In the third passage, God uses the image of the family with God as Father over all of us who believe in Jesus. It's actually the most common picture in the Bible of God's people, and it (like the body illustration) implies that we ought to gather together as a family. Then, as if these others aren't plain enough, God comes right out and says, "Do not neglect the gathering of yourselves together."

Again, I've heard more than a few people say, "I don't go to church because several years ago I had a bad experience at such-and-such church." And I'm sure they're telling the truth: maybe the pastor ran off with one of the women in the church, maybe that person's parents got hurt by somebody else in the church, or whatever. I'm terribly sorry that some people get hurt at the one place where we're supposed to get healing and redemption. But just because someone has a bad experience at *one* church shouldn't keep them from finding a *good* church and getting involved. After all, as an example, there are some bad doctors out there, right? But when you need to see a doctor, do you say, "Well, I had a bad experience at a certain doctor's office, so therefore I'm not going to see any doctor about my sickness"? No. Instead, you go to see a doctor—just not *that* doctor who gave you a bad time. It's the same thing with church, so don't deceive yourself if you've had a bad experience at a particular church: God wants all of his children to gather with other members of the family.

Now that we've gotten some of those excuses out of the way, let's go back to the *why* of gathering together. I mean, why should we gather together at church and such? There are several powerful reasons, so let's mention them here.

First, **we gather to worship God collectively**. As we've already said, there's a certain dynamic to God's presence when we gather collectively. I'm not sure how to explain it fully, but we know with certainty that God manifests his presence when we're gathered together above and beyond how he manifests his presence when we're alone. In addition to Jesus' words in Matthew 18:20 (see above), consider also the words of Psalm 22:3, where it says that God "sits enthroned on the praises" of his people. Naturally, all true Spiritual Athlete Warriors will gather together to worship God.

Second, **we gather to study the Bible**. We already talked about the public study of the Bible. But I might point out one other great aspect of public Bible study, and that is that we can get an explanation of the Bible from others that we couldn't get when we're alone. I like the story in the book of Nehemiah of how the people gathered to study the Bible. After a public reading, this happened:

Then the Levites . . . instructed the people in the Law while the people were [gathered] there. They read from Book of the Law of God, making it clear and giving the meaning so that the people could understand what was being read. (Nehemiah 8:7)

Sometimes it's tough to know exactly what God is saying in the Bible, and that's why God has appointed some of his people to be "pastors and teachers"—so that others might have a better understanding. But you've got to get up and gather in order to receive the teaching, right? And let's not forget that when we gather in a small-group setting to study the Bible, the others in the group help us to interpret circumstances in our lives through the lens of the Bible. That's not a small benefit.

Third, **we gather to encourage one another**. For many folks, this may just be the most meaningful part of gathering. You're sick or going through some kind of difficulty? The friends you gather with will encourage you. You're not sure about a big life-decision you've got to make? The friends you gather with will encourage you. You're feeling alone or emotionally empty? The friends you gather with will encourage you. And let's not forget that when it comes to staying faithful to God, our friends we gather with are supposed to encourage us in this area, too:

> *See to it, brothers and sisters, that none of you has a sinful, unbelieving heart that turns away from the living God. But encourage one another daily, as long as it is called Today, so that none of you may be hardened by the deceitfulness of sin.* (Hebrews 3:13)

Of course, *getting* encouragement is only half of gathering. The other half comes when we're *giving* encouragement. And that requires that we put ourselves in the shoes of those around us rather than standing only (and selfishly) in our own shoes. It means that we must love those we gather with. Or as Peter said, "Love one another deeply" (1 Peter 1:22).

Fourth, **we gather to pool our resources for serving and influencing our neighbors**. In many ways, the most important thing we do together is serving and influencing those around us. We've already stressed in this book that we cannot have a meaningful life apart from having an impact in the lives of others, and when we make it a part of our mission to do that as we gather, we multiply our impact potential. In fact, we've listed these two qualities as separate SAW disciplines because they are so important, so we'll simply say here that our gatherings *must* have an outwardly-focused vision. Otherwise, ultimately, we're wasting our time in gathering. And, by the way, that's a great criteria for thinking about *where* you should gather. That is to say, make sure the place where you're gathering has a broader vision for serving and influencing those who aren't a part of your gathering.

SERVING: Love with Legs on It

One of the greatest temptations in our world today is to seek what theologian Francis Schaeffer called "personal peace," which is the desire "just to be let alone . . . not to be troubled by other people's troubles . . . undisturbed."[4]

I call this the "drawbridge" principle, and it's something that I wrestle with often. You see, I've got my family (my wife and my children) and I've got my job and my possessions. By and large, I've made wise decisions, and now I'm reaping blessings because of it. And, to be totally honest, sometimes I just want to get in my little castle with everything I find meaningful—and then pull up the drawbridge and forget about everybody else. But something inside of me says that there's more to life than *my* happiness, *my* peace, and *my* contentment. And so I lower the drawbridge and go out into the world in order to help other people.

And that's why the discipline I call "serving" is so important for a successful SAW program. See, whenever you engage in the SAW program, it's important to note that Jesus was, is, and always will be the ultimate Spiritual Athlete Warrior—that is, he's the guy we're supposed to be imitating. And when it comes to serving others, Jesus set the ultimate example:

> *The Son of Man [Jesus] did not come to be served, but to serve and to give his life as a ransom for many.* (Mark 10:45)

> *Do nothing out of selfish ambition or vain conceit, but in humility consider others better than yourselves. Each of you should look not only to your own interests, but also to the interests of others. Your attitude should be the same as that of Christ Jesus, who . . . made himself nothing and took the very nature of a servant.* (Philippians 2:3-7)

The key to serving is to focus on other people. It's tough, not least because the human heart—your heart and my heart—is selfish and typically interested only in advancing its own agenda.

Serving focuses primarily upon the temporary physical and emotional needs that others have, and if there was ever a gold-medal winner in this SAW event, it was the woman named Mother Theresa. An Albanian Catholic nun, she founded in 1950 the Missionaries of Charity in Calcutta, India with 13 other nuns. Today, the Missionaries of Charity number more than 4,000 nuns. And though she died in 1997, her legacy continues. In Mother Theresa's own words, the organization's mission statement is to:

> *. . . care for the hungry, the naked, the homeless, the crippled, the blind, the lepers, all those people who feel unwanted, unloved, uncared for throughout society, people that have become a burden to society and are shunned by everyone.*[5]

Fortunately, people like Mother Theresa have led the way. Of course, we don't have to move to Calcutta in order to care for those in need. So let's talk about a couple of practical ways that you can get engaged in the lives of others in order to meet those needs they have.

First, feeding the hungry comes to mind, and there's no shortage of truly hungry people in our world today. There are plenty of opportunities to go to places that feed hungry people and volunteer. But there are other ways that you can serve the hungry without going very far out of your normal routine. For example, have you ever stopped at a red light and seen a person standing there with a sign that says, "Will work for food"—or something like that? What goes through your mind? What do you do? Do you give that person cash and drive away? If so, then he might go find something to drink for dinner. Or what if you actually offer that guy a job of some kind—something temporary, something small? I knew a man in California who actually offered for the guy to come over to his house and do some yard work. And what response did he get? The man said, "Are you crazy? I make $20.00 an hour on this street corner." So should we simply ignore them and drive away? Actually, the best and most expedient idea I've ever seen is to keep some gift certificates to McDonalds or Subway in your glove box and hand one to someone like that. After all, it's probably better for someone to eat dinner with Ronald McDonald than Jack Daniels. It's a simple thing—just one example.

Second, how about befriending the lonely? Did you know that more people are living alone than ever before? In fact, studies show that 27.2 million households in America—that's 25 percent—consist of just one person, compared to 10 percent in 1950.[6] Moreover, the *American Sociological Review* showed recently that the number of people who said they have no personal confidant (that is, a person with whom they can *really* talk) in 2004 was 25 percent, up from 10 percent in 1985.[7] It's easy to overlook these people in the busyness of our own lives. But having an attitude of service helps us to pause and consider those who are hurting and alone.

By the way, let's not forget that when we serve others, we add to our own sense of well-being and fulfillment. After all, there are two kinds of people in this world: the givers and the takers. The takers eat better, but the givers sleep better. And it was Albert Schweitzer who really hit the nail right on the head when it comes to serving: "I don't know what your destiny will be, but one thing I know. The ones among you who will be really happy are those who have sought and found how to serve other people."[8]

INFLUENCING: Impacting Others Spiritually

We're now talking about the need to influence other people for Christ—that is, to influence others to receive Jesus personally by faith and to live their lives for him. We just talked about serving people who are physically or emotionally needy, and we emphasized how that rightly focuses upon the temporary physical and emotional needs that people have. Now we shift our focus to spiritually influencing others, which addresses the spiritual aspect of life.

The need to influence others is pretty obvious, especially when we listen to the words of Jesus:

> *Jesus said to his disciples, "All authority in heaven and on earth has been given to me. Therefore, go and make disciples of all nations, baptizing them in the name of the Father and of the Son and of the Holy Spirit, and teaching them to obey everything I have commanded you. (Matthew 28:18-20)*

> *You will receive power when the Holy Spirit comes on you; and you will be my witnesses in Jerusalem, and in all Judea and Samaria, and to the ends of the earth. (Acts 1:8)*

So what exactly does all of this mean? It means that Jesus wants to us influence others to love, follow, and obey him. And that means that we actively and sincerely engage others on a spiritual level.

"You mean you want us to talk to other people about God? I'm not really into that." I know, I know—most people feel uncomfortable doing that (or at least they *think* they would feel uncomfortable doing that, since most people have never actually done it). And many people get the idea that they've got to go door to door talking to complete and total strangers. But there's much more to spiritually influencing others than that. In fact, you might be surprised at how non-threatening it can be.

So let's look at some ways you can influence people you personally know.

First and foremost, you should **pray for others**, specifically that God would work in their lives. I've found that this is often the most overlooked aspect of influencing other people spiritually. In fact, I've become convinced that it's more important to talk to God about people than to talk to people about God. Both are very important, but effective prayer is what leads to effective influence. So make it a point to pray for those whom you hope to influence for God.

Second, you can **invite others to gather with you** when you gather. This is as easy as saying, "Hey, why don't you come to church with me this Sunday and afterwards we'll get something to eat?" Notice that it doesn't have anything to do with beating someone over the head with a 30-pound Bible or grabbing them by the shirt collar and saying, "Buddy, are you ready to meet God??!!" In fact, this is one of the easiest ways to engage someone else on a spiritual level. And, assuming that you're talking to one of your friends or associates, they'll probably say, "Yes, I'll go with you." In fact, studies have shown that 90 percent of people have said, "If a friend were to invite me to attend church, I would say, 'Yes.'"

Third, **ask others how you can pray for them**. Again, I'm not suggesting that you walk up and down the street with a billboard that says, "TURN OR BURN!" I'm simply saying that you can sincerely ask your friends, neighbors, and others in your sphere of influence how you might be able to pray for them. I've *never* been rejected when asking this question, and you'll be surprised at how many people will lower their defenses and sincerely share their needs with you. Only God knows how their hearts will open up to further influence simply because you asked them how you might pray for them. Of course, once they share their needs with you, be sure to actually pray for them! Certainly, pray for them in your private time of prayer, but (depending on the situation) it's not a bad idea to pray with them right then and there when they tell you their need. Don't forget, it's a great idea to go back and remind them from time to time that you really are praying for them.

A good example of doing this as you go about your daily routine is to ask your waiter or waitress how you can pray for them: "We're about to pray for our meal. How can we pray for you?" We do this on a regular basis in my family, and we've been amazed at how often someone will take just a moment to share their needs. If they can't think of anything immediately, just say, "We'll pray that you get big tips today." But a word of encouragement: if you ask the waiter or waitress how you can pray for them, please be sure to leave a BIG tip. After all, once you've identified yourself as a Christian, the last thing you want to do is leave a bad impression with a meager tip!

Fourth, take an opportunity to **tell others your own story**. And what do I mean by that? I'm talking about sharing with someone else how you became a Christian—that is, how you personally accepted Christ into your life. And this is a great time to recall Jesus' words in Acts 1:8 (mentioned above), where he said, "You shall be my witnesses." Yes, Jesus expects us to be witnesses. And what is a witness? Well, as Adrian Rogers often said, "A witness simply tells what he's seen and heard." You see, many people get the idea that Jesus expects us to his *lawyers* rather than his witnesses—that is, they think we have to argue with other people and try to coerce them to accept a certain perspective. But look again at Jesus' own words: "You shall be my *witnesses*." So

Jesus expects us to share with other people a word about what we've seen and heard. And how easy is that? It's very easy—assuming, of course, that you've seen and heard something in your own life.

So what's a good plan for sharing your story? It's not very complicated, and anyone can share their story in about 2 minutes. First, talk a little bit about your life before you accepted Christ. Then talk about how you accepted Christ. And finally, talk a little bit about how Jesus has impacted your life. It's best to write it out and get a handle on it before you try to share it with someone else without notes. Then you'll have it tucked away in your heart and mind and can recall it when an opportunity arises to tell someone else "what you've seen and heard."

Need an example? Here's my story in a nutshell:

I grew up going to church all my life—just about every Sunday. But I really didn't have a relationship with God. In fact, it was more like "go to church on Sunday and live like hell the rest of the week." But then in April 1990, just about the time I turned seventeen, a couple of friends invited me to go to their youth group. Well, they had free food and good-looking girls, so how could I refuse? So I went for a few weeks. Now, this church encouraged everyone to read the Bible for themselves, which was something I had never done. So I began to get into the Bible. And I began to see that we're all separated from God because of our personal sin, that Jesus died on the cross so that we could have our sins forgiven and have a relationship with God, and that God's gift of forgiveness is available to anyone who deliberately turns from their sin and personally accepts Christ into their lives. And I said to God, "I've always believed in you and thought that the Bible was important, but I don't think I've ever personally asked Jesus to come into my life." So that's exactly what I did—I asked Jesus Christ to come into my life and to forgive my sin.

And that's when everything changed for me. My life went from "go to church on Sunday and live like hell the rest of the week" to a relationship with God where I wanted to live for him all week long. And I've been blessed beyond belief: I would simply say that I couldn't be the man, the husband, the father, and the minister that I am today if I hadn't asked Jesus Christ to come into my life when I was seventeen years old as I did.

It's just that simple. And I can't tell you how many times I've been able to share that story with others over the years—I've been able to tell others what I've seen and heard.

SAW: Get After It!

Remember the SAW challenge at the beginning of this chapter? Here it is again:

Train yourselves to be godly. For physical exercise has some value, but godliness has value for all things, holding promise both for this present life and the life to come. (1 Timothy 4:7-8)

As we've already said, this chapter, in many ways, is the epicenter of the whole book. Anyone who wants to be a more elite man must understand the principles in this chapter. In other words, a man cannot excel in life without understanding the spiritual disciplines of studying, praying, gathering, serving, and influencing. And the SAW program can help every man touch upon each of these disciplines.

Hopefully, you've gotten some very practical and applicable ideas here for training yourself in godliness. Going to the spiritual gym pays huge dividends. So get spiritually ripped, go to the spiritual gym and get big, and you'll see for yourself the value for this life and for the life to come, eternal life.

7

Your Dad's Leadership:
The Good, the Bad, and the Ugly

Stu Weber once said, "The word 'dad' is one of the most powerful words in the English language, because it brings up many emotions and memories."[1]

There's a lot of truth in that statement, right?

This chapter is all about coming to grips with the relationships that we have with our dads, whether they are (or were) good, bad, or ugly. In addition, this chapter is all about endeavoring to be the right kind of dad to the children that we have or someday will have.

Admittedly, I've got some housekeeping to do for myself in this matter. Do you remember how I talked highly about my grandfather, John Dillin, earlier in the book? He was, in my estimation, a man who knew "the great enthusiasms." Well, my dad was kind of the opposite of my grandfather. Harold Kramer was a hard worker, and everyone who knew him would agree. He worked long hours—first in, last out. And I'm very grateful for how he provided for our family. But as I look back over his life, I see a lot of *existence* but I don't see a lot of *life*. (Remember how we earlier noted the difference between the two?) My dad was the kind of guy who got up every morning, drank his coffee, went to work, came home, ate dinner, watched the news, and went to bed. Period. As a result, unfortunately, my dad never really connected with anyone emotionally, not me, not my brother, not even my mom . . . nobody. I believe that his was a lonely existence, made more difficult by an alcoholism that led to two ruined marriages and the loss of a job he had for almost twenty years. It's hard to say it, but there were days when I was a child when I wished he wouldn't come home. Was he a *bad* man? No, I don't think so. But he was far from being a more elite man—"a more elite dad."

Let's do this: let's talk about some fundamental issues related to fatherhood, let's talk in terms of what "right looks like," and let's also not forget to talk about how, at the end of the day—regardless of whatever relationship we have with our earthly fathers—we all have a heavenly Father who has proven himself to be a "father to the fatherless."

Some Fundamentals

I doubt any man reading this book would disagree with what we're going to talk about at this point—namely, that dads are *essential* and that dads are *influential*. Just ask anyone who never knew their dad and they'll tell you it's true.

Dads are Essential

Let's talk about how essential dads really are, because there are numerous voices who say they're optional. In the late 80s and early 90s, a guy named Dan Quayle was Vice President of the United States. At that time, a popular television sitcom titled "Murphy Brown" attempted to normalize the fatherless family as just as ideal as the traditional "nuclear" family with a mom and a dad. Well, Dan Quayle publically questioned the wisdom of that line of thought portrayed in the show. As a result, Quayle was roasted from coast the coast for his comments. Ironically, after the dust had settled a few years later, most came out and agreed with Quayle's comments, to include President Bill Clinton as well as Candice Bergen, the actress who played the "Murphy Brown" title character.[2] More recently, the actress Jennifer Aniston starred in the movie "The Switch," portraying a single woman who chooses artificial insemination in order to have a child. In commenting about the movie, she stated that men are optional in child raising and that "the concept of the family has evolved beyond the traditional stereotype defined by a mother, father, two children, and a dog named Spot."[3]

These are both specific examples from the Hollywood sub-culture, and some might call them isolated. But they represent a broader perspective that questions the value of having a man around to influence and even lead the family. Fortunately, large numbers of people have seen through these misguided premises, such as Wendy Wright of the group Concerned Women for America: "Children need a dad. Traditional family values may be boring for Hollywood celebrities, but they nevertheless develop stable, secure, and healthy people."[4]

This disregard for fatherhood is rooted in a deeper issue, and that issue is the radical feminist philosophy that tells women that they shouldn't depend on a man for anything, let alone to be the father of their children. For example, in a recent book entitled *The Feminine Mistake*, writer Leslie Bennetts warns women everywhere that they must learn to live independently from men if they are to experience fulfillment and happiness. To illustrate her point, she tells the story of how, back in the 1930s, her grandfather abandoned her grandmother after the couple had been married for 10 years, leaving her grandmother to fend for herself and their children.[5] I truly hate that her family had to endure such pain. But it's ironic that she reads her family's experience into the potential future of every woman by essentially saying, "Hey girls, this is what happened to my grandmother; it will probably happen to you, too. So just go ahead and throw the men under the bus—who needs them anyway?" Incidentally, this story gives insight into what *really* drives the radical feminist agenda—namely, bad experiences with dead-beat men. (By the way, this should be a significant lesson for all you men reading this book: "Are you going to be another reason for a woman to jettison her God-given capacity for a meaningful relationship with a man, or are you going to be the kind of man your wife *needs*?")

So do we really need fathers in our lives? Hey, who are we kidding? Fathers are *essential* to the raising of solid boys and girls. Consider what often happens when fathers are absent in the lives of their children. Tony Dungy's fantastic "All Pro Dad" organization has often highlighted the need for fathers: 90% of homeless or runaway children are from fatherless homes, 85% of children who exhibit behavioral disorders are from fatherless homes, 85% of all youths in prison grew up in fatherless homes, and 80% of rapists are from fatherless homes.[5] Having a dad in the picture isn't magic, but it really does make a difference.

Dads are Influential

Nobody needs to be reminded that dads are very influential in the lives of their children, whether for the good or for the bad. Oftentimes, dads have a very powerful and positive influence on their kids—and on their sons especially. Unfortunately, some dads have a negative influence on their kids. Either way, the influence cannot be denied.

Here's one example. I was listening to the "Dan Patrick Show" recently on the radio, and Dan was talking to Bill Madden, long-time sportswriter for the *New York Daily News* and author of *Steinbrenner: The Last Lion of Baseball*.[6] The conversation turned to the book, and Dan asked Madden about George Steinbrenner's legendary temper and rough treatment of his employees. To my surprise, Madden began to highlight the relationship that Steinbrenner had with his father.

As the story goes, Henry Steinbrenner, George's dad, had an amazing resume: MIT honors student, champion low hurdles athlete, and naval architect. But his rigorous self-expectations and demands translated into unbelievable pressure on his son with endless school assignments, hurdles practice, music lessons, work, and so forth— George would later recall, "My dad was one tough German."[7] When the younger Steinbrenner attended Williams College and ran track, his father repeatedly berated him both for his performance on the track *and* the fact that he didn't gain admission to MIT. As one of George's friends later recalled, "The fear George had of his father was amazing. He had to call his father after every track meet, and inevitably his father would be ticked off because he didn't do better. I thought his father was a nasty guy."[8] In 1978, after George had success, fame, and untold wealth, he built a new stadium at MIT in honor of his father. But when he brought his father to the dedication ceremony, the elder Steinbrenner brusquely said, "That's the only way you'd ever get into *this* school!"[9]

So how did this toxic relationship impact George's life? Did he determine to be a better man than his dad? Not hardly. George Steinbrenner was famously abusive and unreasonably demanding toward employees, arguably due in large part to a lack of affirmation from his father. Sadly, a close friend recalled, "George was permanently scarred by his father's rigidity, and I have no doubt he'd have given up all his championship rings just to have gotten a hug and an 'I love you, son' from the old man. The sad part is that he treated his own kids the same way.'"[10] We're going to unpack some of this stuff later in the chapter, but I hope you sense the powerful (*albeit* negative) influence that Henry Steinbrenner had on his son George.

Now, how about a *positive* example? It's a brief one but, at least for me, it's very powerful. My grandfather, John Dillin, often spoke of his dad. There are only two things specifically I remember about what he said, but they are both burned into my heart. First, I can remember on several occasions when he said, "My dad was my *best friend.*" Short statement; no flourishes. But I'll never forget it, probably because I wish that I could have said that about my dad and probably also because I want to be the kind of dad about whom my kids say the same thing. Or, as Adrian Rogers often said, "I want my kids to think that George Washington and Abraham Lincoln were the Jesse James boys compared to their daddy!"[11] I don't remember a lot of the details about the relationship between my grandfather and his dad, but it must have been a powerful relationship. Also, I specifically remember my grandfather saying, "I'm going to be buried in Sebring, Florida, right next to my dad." Wow, who says that kind of stuff these days?!

Well, the take away is obvious, isn't it? Dads are essential and, for better or for worse, their influence is powerful. You might have been blessed by a dad who was there for you in a powerful way; or you might not have enjoyed that blessing. Either way, we're going to begin to see how we can set ourselves up for success as dads in our own right.

Here's What Right Looks Like

Eric Ludy, author of *God's Gift to Women*, has noted, "As young men, sometimes we all need a picture of what we *could* become." Or, as we sometimes say in the Army, we need someone to show us "what right looks like."[12]

I'd like to talk about the big picture in two broad ways: the concept of "blessing" and the concept of "legacy." Again, remember that we're talking about coming to grips with the relationship we have (or had) with our own dads as well as the relationships that we someday will have with our kids. So let's think in those terms as we talk about the "blessing" and the "legacy."

The Blessing

What do I mean when I talk about the "blessing?" I'm talking about a sense of acceptance, affirmation, and love that a child receives from a dad who is wise enough and sensitive to give it.

Consider the story in the Bible of Isaac and his sons Jacob and Esau to illustrate the point (Genesis 27:1-40). In the story, Isaac is an old man on his death bed, and he prepares to give a "blessing" to his oldest son, Esau. In that culture, there was a special word of affirmation as well as tangible benefits that were conveyed upon the oldest son by the father, and Isaac wanted to provide just such a blessing to his son. But Jacob, who was the younger brother, sought to get the blessing before Esau. So, after Esau went out of the house, Jacob disguised himself to resemble (and even smell like) Esau in order to trick his father, who had poor vision and lacked the ability to identify his son clearly. So, unknown to Isaac, Jacob received this special blessing. And as a result, upon learning that he did not get the blessing, Esau was devastated.

You know, the human heart has not really changed over thousands of years. Every man yearns for the "blessing," whether he realizes it or not. James MacDonald puts it this way:

Every person longs for the blessing. Deep within the heart of every person is a longing for parental approval—for a confidence in knowing that our parents know us, love us, and are proud of us. We search for it our whole lives. From the pre-schooler who calls out from the sandbox, "Dad, Dad! Look what I've made!" to the young child who fidgets and bows nervously as mom reads the report card to the high-schooler who stands in the kitchen dressed for the prom saying, "Daddy, how do I look?" to the adult who can't wait for mom and dad to see the new house or to hear about the new job.[13]

John Trent and Gary Smalley, in their book entitled *The Blessing*, point to dads who lovingly give spoken words of affirmation, meaningful touch, and the casting of a spiritual vision for their children.[14] I'd have to agree that they've got a powerful formula for giving the blessing. And I think it's important to mention how dads can (and should) affirm their children—especially their boys.

First, dads should affirm their kids verbally. I don't know about you, but I could probably count on one hand the number of times my dad ever said to me, "I love you." Maybe it was just a generational thing, but children of every generation want to hear those words.

Beyond that fundamental proclamation, let's also think about how dads ought to affirm their children with acceptance. Too often dads expect perfection, and when they don't find it they go out of their way to berate their child's efforts—remember George Steinbrenner? Maybe you had a demanding dad and are even now wondering if you really, truly had his acceptance.

A great story about this kind of affirmation is found in the Hebrew culture of the Bible days. Evidently, Hebrew boys around ages 13-14 commonly received this kind of blessing. A Hebrew father would gather several of his peers and friends in a circle, place his child in the center, and then the adults would give words of counsel and affirmation to the child. Then, in a culmination of the event, the father would take his child up on his shoulders, dance around, and say publicly to all of his friends, "This is my beloved son, in whom I am well pleased." (That might sound familiar to you, because it's what God said publicly on the day that Jesus was baptized in Mark 1:11.)

Beyond verbal affirmation, let's not forget that dads should affirm their kids physically—that is, with their touch. I'm afraid to say that many dads are severely constipated on this issue. Too many dads are unwilling to hug and kiss their children on a regular basis. Now, men in my dad's generation did not do this very well—I certainly didn't get a lot of it. But the current generation of dads is at least beginning to discover this very important issue. Maybe you got this, and maybe you didn't. But I doubt anyone doesn't agree with what right looks like.

Maybe you're reading this and you're saying, "Yeah, I guess I got the 'blessing' when I was a kid." Or, on the other hand, maybe you didn't. Either way, it's a great time to remind ourselves what happens when kids don't get the "blessing" from their dads. This will help us to honestly assess the relationship we had with our dad and also to help us determine to be for our children kind of the dads that they deserve.

And let's not forget that without a warm, loving, and affectionate relationship with their fathers, children often go looking for that affection in other places. In my own counseling and ministry, I have never seen a sexually disoriented person who had a warn and affectionate relationship with their father.

So, overall, do you think that George Steinbrenner ever got the "blessing" from his dad? I seriously doubt it, and I suppose that it had a very negative impact on George.

Why Withhold the Blessing?

By the way, any idea why some dads withhold the blessing from their kids? In the days of Isaac, Jacob, and Esau, there was technically only one "blessing" to give—and it normally went to the eldest son. But in our world today, a dad can give an equal blessing to each of his children.

So if there's not limitations on the blessing today, why do dads so commonly withhold this important gift?

First and foremost, dads often withhold the blessing because they never received it themselves. The irony is that these men who never received it still long for it well into their adult lives, yet they are often totally oblivious to the fact that they aren't giving it to their own kids. Maybe they *think* they are, but in fact they are not. As a family counselor and student of human relationships, if I've seen this scenario once I've seen it a thousand times. So, if you're a dad, seriously ask yourself this question: "Did *I* get the 'blessing' from my dad? Am *I* giving the blessing to my children?"

Second, dads often withhold the blessing because they are goal- oriented men who often neglect those things that they already "have in hand" in order to focus upon what they don't possess but want to gain. This is certainly true for many husbands who neglect the relationships they already have with their wives in favor of accomplishing more and more at work. And it frequently carries over to a man's relationship with his children.

Third, let's not forget that some dads, believe it or not, are just kind of embarrassed by their children. After all, a man takes years to build *his* reputation, *his* position, *his* wealth, and *his* place in this world—only to find that his child doesn't follow in his footsteps or doesn't make the same decisions that he did. In cases like that, the dad often demonstrates that he's more concerned about himself than about his child. In fact, this kind of dad, instead of blessing his child with affirmation and acceptance, often curses his child with ridicule and neglect.

When the Blessing is Withheld

What happens when the blessing is withheld? What happens in the lives of those children who don't get it? I've seen a few trends to include some in my own life, so here are some ideas.

First, when the blessing is withheld, children naturally try harder and harder to get it. Again, the story of George Steinbrenner is so relevant here. He went to great lengths to succeed in life, and one can easily see both in his own words and in the words of those who knew him best that he was continually seeking his dad's approval and affirmation. Oftentimes, men who pursue the blessing with more exertion and greater work intensity don't realize what they're doing. Unfortunately, all of this extra effort and energy only adds to the disappointment.

Second, men who don't get the blessing from their own dads tend to seek affirmation from other older men—that is, they begin to look at other men as a father figure in hopes of getting some kind of affirmation from them. There's nothing wrong with this, per se. However, it often becomes an endless search for what should have been and could have been the real thing.

The Legacy

Your relationship with your dad might have been hell on earth—or maybe it's still hell on earth. I would be willing to guess that the majority of men reading this book have some unresolved issues with their dads. So what are we going to do about it?

The most important thing to do is to make it right to the best of your ability. If your dad is still alive, then do whatever you can to love him and cultivate the kind of relationship you want to have with him. If he is no longer alive, then at least make it right in your own heart.

Beyond making it right, you've got to *draw a line in the sand* and purpose in your heart that you will learn from the relationship that was less than ideal and then be the dad for your kids that you didn't have. I've done that in my own life and I would encourage you to do that, too. I've often said to myself:

That generation had their opportunity and made their decisions; now it's my turn to make the most of the opportunity that God has given me, and I'm not going to throw it away.

You may say, "That sounds good, but I feel like I'm destined to make the same mistakes that my dad made." That's a pretty common argument. But I want you to know that regardless of who went before you and what they did, you have full freedom to draw that line in the sand and be the man you know you should be.

There's a great story in the Bible about what I call the "legacy principle." It's basically the story of three generations of men and how each successive man turned out. It's found in the book of Ezekiel, chapter 18, and it starts out by a popular proverb that the people were evidently using all over the place:

> *The word of the Lord came to me: "What do you people mean by quoting this proverb all over the land of Israel: 'The fathers eat sour grapes, and the children's teeth are set on edge'?"* (Ezekiel 18:1-2)

See, the people were basically saying, "Our dads did such and such, and now we can't help it that we're doing the same thing." They were making excuses for their own foolishness based upon their fathers' foolishness.

On the one hand, it's true that we're all influenced by our parents, and sometimes those influences run deep in our own hearts to the point that they're difficult to shake. I got that. But listen to how God demonstrates that each of us is free to build our own lives, regardless of what previous generations said or did:

> *Suppose there is a righteous man who does what is right. He does not worship idols . . . he does not defile his neighbor's wife . . . [and] he does not oppress anyone. That man is righteous, declares the Lord.* (Ezekiel 18:5-9)

OK, so here's the first man, and he's a good man. But how did his son turn out?

> *Suppose he has a violent son who . . . defiles his neighbor's wife . . . oppresses the needy . . . commits robbery . . . [and] worships idols. Will such a man live? He will not!* (Ezekiel 18:10-13)

So now the son is a real dead beat. Evidently, he didn't follow his dad's example and life. It was *his* decision to make, and *he* made it.

Now, you might think that his son (the good man's grandson) would also turn out to be rotten. But, to everyone's surprise, he goes in the opposite direction and chooses to do what's right . . . in spite of his dad's bad example

> *But suppose this son has a son who sees all the sins that his father commits, and though he sees them, he does not do such things. He does not worship idols . . . does not defile his neighbor's wife . . . does not commit robbery . . . but gives food to the hungry . . . [and] withholds his hand from sin. He will not die for this father's sin; he will surely live.* (Ezekiel 18:14-18)

Here's the good-news story: this young man considered his father's ways (as well as his relationship with his dad), and he decided to draw a line in the sand and go in the other direction.

That should give *all* of us hope.

A Father to the Fatherless

In July 2010, the largest man-hunt in the history of Britain ended as Raoul Moat, who had recently shot his ex-girlfriend, her new boyfriend, and a British police officer, shot himself after a 6-hour standoff with police. An emotionally-disturbed individual, Moat carried on sporadic conversation with police during the ordeal. One eyewitness said, "I don't remember a lot of what was said, but one thing really stands out in my mind, and that was when he said, 'I've no dad haven't got a dad, no one cares about me.'"[16]

Moat's sense of "fatherlessness" doesn't excuse his actions, but it once again gives a sense that fathers are important and that the absence of fathers is part of what's wrong with our world today. It's no wonder that a recent Gallup Poll showed that, when asked "What is the most significant family or social problem facing America today?" no less than 79% of those polled answered "the physical absence of a father in the home."[17]

Let's face it: some men will never receive their father's blessing and affirmation. No matter how hard they try, they will always feel this pain. But does that leave them with nothing. By no means!

One of the greatest words to describe God throughout the Bible is the word "Father." In the gospel of John, for example, Jesus referred to God no less than 110 times as "Father." And consider these important verses from the book of Psalms:

God is a father to the fatherless; he sets the lonely in families (Psalm 68:5-6)

Though my father . . . forsakes me, the Lord will receive me (Psalm 27:10)

These words of wisdom will likely resonate with everyone, but especially with those who did not get a "blessing" from their dads. I know they do with me. What about you?

And let's not forget that one of the most powerful pictures of God's love for us in the Bible is that of adoption. You see, the image in the Bible is that God is the Father and Jesus Christ is his "one and only son." Yet, everyone who comes to God by faith in Jesus is "adopted" into the family—that is, he or she becomes a "child of

God" as well as an adopted brother or sister of Christ himself. Hear these words:

> *Those who are led by the Spirit of God are children of God. For you received . . . the spirit of adoption, through which we cry "Abba, Father." The Spirit himself testifies with our spirits that we are children of God. Now if we are children, then we are heirs—heirs of God and co-heirs with Christ.* (Romans 8:14-17)

It's significant to note that the language used here, "Abba, Father," was a way that children called out to their fathers in those days. It would be like a child saying "Daddy" in today's language. It's denotes love and a recognition of an authentic relationship not clouded by pretense or conflict.

So what does all of this mean? It means that, regardless of whatever kind of relationship we might have (or had) with our earthly fathers, there is a Father who loves each of us more than we could ever know and more than any earthly father could possibly love us. Even after more than 25 years of walking with God, I can still barely get my mind wrapped around it—it's just that awesome!

Think About It

We've all got some thinking to do, don't we? Some of you men don't even want to "go there" on the topic of your dad. But it's important that we get a handle on the issue, not just for our own well-being but also for the sake of the children we have (or will have someday). We owe it to ourselves and we owe it to them to sort through these issues.

8

Give Way Together: The Commander's Intent for Your Marriage

The U.S. Army Ranger School consists of three phases lasting between three to four weeks each: the Benning phase at Fort Benning Georgia, the mountain phase in Dahlonega, Georgia, and the Florida phase at Eglin Air Force Base, Florida. Each phase has distinct training objectives and geographical characteristics. The Benning phase focuses on patrolling basics in the piney Georgia woods. The mountain phase features technical climbing and patrolling over mountainous terrain. The Florida phase features patrolling through swamps and flooded terrain.

The Florida phase also features water movements up and down the Yellow River in rigid rubber boats called Zodiacs. Throughout the phase, a total of seven students pile into each Zodiac boat. Three paddle on one side, three paddle on another side, and the seventh student oversees the paddling from the stern—no outboard motors allowed! The student at the stern, known as the coxswain, calls commands to guide the boat. If he wants the boat to bear left, he says, "Right side give way!" The students on the right side of the boat paddle while those on the left side refrain from paddling, and the boat slowly turns left. If he wants the boat to bear right, he says, "Left side give way!" The students on the left side of the boat paddle while those on the right side refrain from paddling, and the boat slowly turns right. If the coxswain wants the boat to go forward, he says, "All give way together!" All sides paddle together in unison, and the boat advances down the river in a forward direction. It's a classic illustration of coordinated teamwork.

It's also an excellent illustration of God's intent for marriage. "All give way together" is a great strategy for a husband and wife working together in unison to move their marriage down the river of life. Selfishness is the number-one marriage killer, but selfless husbands and wives make for great marriages. This chapter is meant to equip you, the husband, with a vision for selfless leadership in your marriage that you and your wife might ultimately give way together.

Husbands have a God-given responsibility to selflessly lead their families, beginning with their marriages. In order to lead selflessly, the husband must first receive and understand the "commander's intent"—that is, what God says about marriage in the Bible. Next, he must set the pace for his marriage in accordance with that intent. And that pace must create conditions for he and his wife to work together as a single unit. Consider God's first command about marriage in the entire Bible:

> *Therefore a man shall leave his father and his mother and hold fast to his wife, and they shall become one flesh.* (Genesis 2:24)

Moreover, consider these important words about marriage, especially given to husbands, from the New Testament:

> *Submit to one another out of reverence to Christ. . . . Husbands, love your wives as Christ loved the church and gave himself up*

for her, that he might sanctify her . . . that she might be holy and without blemish. (Ephesians 5:21, 25-27)

These two key Bible passages provide a template for husbands to set the physical, emotional, and spiritual pace in their marriages. That pace must be one of selfless leadership and servant leadership. When a husband delivers on that, the couple is better equipped to "give way together" and move forward in a healthy and God-blessed way.

There are four words that capture the essence of the Bible passages listed above and characterize a husband's role as selfless leader in his marriage: (1) Priority, (2) Commitment, (3) Intimacy, and (4) Love. In this chapter, we'll consider each of these.

Priority

The first thing we see in God's intent for marriage is that it is a relationship that should have priority over all other relationships: " . . . a man shall leave his father and his mother." Marriage is the most significant relationship of emotional and physical closeness that a man can have in this life. This intent clearly shows that a man's marriage is to be more important than his relationship with his parents. But implied in this intent is the idea that a man's marriage should take priority over all other relationships, too. In fact, the only relationship that should eclipse a man's marriage is his relationship with God. After all, God was in Adam's life even before Eve came along.

Speaking of priority, I once heard about a man who bought a parakeet at the pet store that was guaranteed to talk. He took the bird home and put the cage on the table, but the bird didn't talk. After a few days, he went back to the pet store and complained, "The bird isn't talking!" The manager said, "You mean the bird climbed up and down the ladder and he still didn't talk?" The man asked, "What ladder?" The manager replied, "He won't talk until he climbs up and down the ladder—and you can buy one for five dollars." So the man bought the ladder. A few days later, he was back in the store saying, "The bird still won't talk." The manager said, "You mean the bird went up and down the ladder and pecked the little bell and still won't talk?" The man asked, "What bell?!" The manager explained, "You need to buy a bell. It only costs 10 dollars." So the man bought the bell. Then, later in the week, he came back and said angrily, "The bird is NOT talking!!" So the manager said, "So he used the ladder, pecked the bell, and looked at himself in the mirror and still didn't talk?" The man, almost losing his mind, said, "WHAT MIRROR?" The manager said, "You can buy one for only 15 dollars." So the man bought the mirror and stomped out of the shop. The next week, he came back, and the manager asked, "Is the bird talking?" The man said, "No, the bird is dead!" The manager replied, "You mean he didn't say anything at all?" And the man said, "Well, he did say one thing. Right before he died, he said, 'Don't they have any birdseed down at that store?!'"

The main point of that silly little story is this: It's very easy in life to pile all sorts of things and activities and endeavors on our plates, only to find out that the most important things have dried up and died on the vine. It's certainly a great illustration and warning for marriages everywhere. After 20 years of marriage and relationship counseling I've observed that marriages struggle when the marriage is not at or near the top of the couple's priority list.

On that note, what do your life's priorities look like? Have you ever taken the time to list your priorities—that is, take out a sheet of paper and a pen, then make a list of your life's priorities? And where does your marriage stack up on that list? For me, the list looks like this:

- Pilgrim (GOD)
- Partner (WIFE)

- Parent (KIDS)
- Professional (JOB)
- Player (LEISURE)

There's so much we could say about this list, but let's just zero in on the place of marriage and say, bottom line up front, that your marriage, except for your relationship with God, should be the most important thing to you on this entire earth. Or, to put it another way, your marriage is meant to outlast everything else in life.

That's an important reminder for men everywhere, not least because our goal as husbands is to lead our marriages and families to go the distance and finish well. In many ways, that's becoming harder and more difficult than ever. Consider this text from a recent New York Time's article:

> *Late divorce (also called 'silver' or 'gray' divorce) is becoming more common and more acceptable. In 2014, people age 50 and above were twice as likely to divorce than in 1990. For those over 65, the increase was even higher. At the same time, divorce rates have plateaued or dropped among other age groups. Take Al and Tipper Gore for example. They split in 2010 after 40 years of marriage and four children together.*[1]

How do these "late divorces" happen? In most cases, couples have been distracted by all manner of things over the years—raising children, careers, leisure pursuits, and so forth—and have put their marriages on cruise control without deliberately investing in their relationships. Then, when a lot of those distractions begin to taper off, the couple realizes that they have no relationship left and they call it quits. It's often said, "Most marriages don't end over a blowout, they end over a slow leak."

Given that we can't take anything for granted in marriage, the marriage priority means that you as a husband must invest in your marriage, as Dave Ramsey would put it, with a "gazelle intensity." In other words, your marriage should truly be a "no-fail" mission in your heart, your mind, and your life. That means that you're willing to invest energy, resources, and time into your marriage—whatever it takes.

Commitment

Second, let's also consider the concept of commitment. As mentioned already, if marriages that struggle often have a misplaced view on relationship priorities, I've observed on the other hand that those marriages that go the distance and finish well have a rock-solid conviction about commitment.

Genesis 2:24 says that a husband is to "hold fast" to his wife. The Hebrew word translated as "hold fast" is a very interesting word (some Bible translations say "united to" or "embraces" or even "cleave"). It occurs 14 times in the Old Testament, most often to speak of a relentless, determined devotion to someone, some task, or some thing. It can refer to devotion within human relationships (for example, Ruth 1:14 – "Ruth clung to Naomi"). It can refer to a relentless pursuit of something or a particular task (for example, Judges 20:45, where one army relentlessly pursued another). In Genesis 2:24, it envisions what Special Forces Chaplain Jeff Hawkins often calls "an unshakeable, unbreakable" marriage based on commitment.

Here's something every husband must remember: people get married because of emotions, but they stay married because of commitment. You see, emotions are like the waves of the ocean— sometimes they're up and sometimes they're down. Or, as someone once said, "The ship of marriage sails on the ocean of emotion." (Truth be told, we sometimes get a little seasick on that ocean, don't we?) Of course, we all love the romantic emotions that come with marriage, don't we? After all, as Tommy Nelson has said, "Without romantic emotions, all you've got is a maid married to a butler—a business contract."[2] And who wants their marriage simply to be a business contract? But you cannot bank on your emotions holding your marriage together. After all, when the emotions are low, what do you have? You have your commitment.

Here's some truth in advertising at this point: there were days early in my marriage when I didn't even LIKE my wife! (And she didn't like me, either.) So what did we have at that point? We had commitment. In fact, I've often told my wife, "If you ever leave me, I'm going with you!"

A more elite man shouldn't have difficulty understanding this concept of commitment, not least because the Ranger Creed says, "Surrender is not a Ranger word." It's not hard to see that divorce is like surrender, and Rangers recoil at the mere thought of surrender. Of course, that sounds great, but it's a lot harder to accomplish and maintain. After all, commitment means that a man must live with his wife not only when she is at her very best, but also when she is at her very worst. I often tell couples, "Marriage is like buying a record. You buy it for what's on side A and you just put up with side B."

Intimacy

Third, let's consider the concept of intimacy. When Genesis 2:24 says that "the two shall become one flesh," men everywhere are thinking, "Finally, you got to my favorite part!" And it's true, our first thoughts is toward the physical intimacy that rightly goes along with marriage. But keep in mind that intimacy is a three-dimensional proposition that transcends the physical relationship—there's physical intimacy, emotional intimacy, and spiritual intimacy.

When we talk about "intimacy," we're primarily talking about closeness. The word "intimacy" comes from the Latin word *intimus*, which means "inmost part." Or as relationship expert Jill Savage has said, "Intimacy is defined as 'in-to-me-see'—that is, true intimacy involves honesty, transparency, and voluntary vulnerability."[3] All three dimensions of intimacy are meant to feed into this state of closeness between a husband and wife.

Now let's be clear about the background of this intimacy. Look back at Genesis 2:18-23. Here we see Adam naming the animals. I'm certain at first he was very excited about naming all of these interesting creatures. But he began to notice something that did not put him at ease. He saw that Mr. Horse had a Mrs. Horse, Mr. Bird had a Mrs. Bird, Mr. Elephant had a Mrs. Elephant, and Mr. Bird had a Mrs. Bird. And through this process, he became very aware that there was a Mr. Adam but there was no Mrs. Adam. We might say the he even got a little frustrated! God was not happy with this situation, either, so he created someone "corresponding" or "suited" to Adam—he created Eve. And when Eve showed up, Adam said, "This at last is bone of my bones and flesh of my flesh." But that loses something in translation. A better translation of the Hebrew is something like, "FINALLY, someone like ME!"

If that story informs intimacy in our marriages, then we as husbands need to invest in such a way as to cultivate closeness with our wives across the physical, emotional, and spiritual spectrums. But that can be a difficult task given some of the roadblocks to intimacy we face on a regular basis. So, for the sake of men everywhere, let's highlight a few of those roadblocks and help men to overcome them.

Selfishness

First and foremost, the biggest roadblock to physical intimacy is selfishness. Selfishness disrupts physical intimacy more than any other roadblock—in fact, selfishness is the number-one marriage killer across the board. For example, when a husband deceives himself into thinking that physical intimacy is all about his pleasure, he's wrong, yet that's a massive roadblock over which many men stumble and fall.

A case in point is the battle with pornography, which, in many ways, is a battle against selfishness. Let's just assume that a man's wife is opposed to his looking at pornography. That's not always true, but it's true in the overwhelming majority of cases—and it's very reasonable for a wife to object to pornography in her husband's life. After all, pornography does nothing to help a husband make and maintain his commitment in marriage. The images in pornography show a man going from one woman to the next, sometimes even with multiple woman at the same time. The battle for men to maintain their marital commitment is hard enough without that kind of messaging, so it's easy to see why a wife would be opposed to it. And on top of that, pornography degrades the women in general and our wives in particular. The kind of things that men do to women in pornography is unspeakably degrading, and if the women weren't being paid a great deal of money they most likely wouldn't consent to it (unless they had some warped sexual addiction or mental illness—and that's not uncommon, either). I heard a woman formerly employed in the pornography industry talk about how many women came to Hollywood to get into the business. Evidently, a large number of women make one movie, but very few return for a second. Why? Because even they were shocked at how degrading pornography can be. And let's not forget that wives also feel degraded when their husbands look at pornography. Think about it: many women are already self-conscious about their appearance; how does a wife feel when her husband is lusting after another woman who's probably had numerous procedures to enhance her physical appearance? In many cases, the husband chooses to look at pornography even after his wife has voiced her concern and opposition. That is a classic scenario in this battle with selfishness.

Beyond pornography, how about the battle with selfishness in the marriage bedroom. I hate to say it but the stereotype is not entirely unfounded: husbands are in it to get theirs, roll over, and go to sleep. That's not intimacy, that's ecstasy. And while there's nothing wrong with ecstasy, the overall idea is that a husband should be more concerned with his wife's ecstasy than his own. That's what I learned as a newly-married man.

Let's take a trip back in time to the year 2000. I was 27 years old and engaged to be married. Due to my spiritual convictions—and a huge dose of God's grace!—I had never been with a woman sexually. So you might imagine that I was very eager for the honeymoon to arrive. But I also didn't have much of a philosophy on sex. In fact, I pretty much assumed I was going to get to the honeymoon and go in there like the Marines hitting the beach—"Take no prisoners!!" But fortunately about a month before I got married, someone gave me a book that, even among Christians, almost sounds a little corny today: *How to Get Your Sex Life Off to a Great Start.*[4] I read that book and my eyes were opened. It basically said that a husband's goal is to seek his wife's pleasure and a wife's goal is to seek her husband's pleasure. I have gotten a lot of mileage out of that basic philosophy over the years. In fact, oftentimes when I speak at a marriage conference, I refer to my wife as "the most sexually-satisfied" wife in attendance (with her permission, of course). And then I go on to explain what I mean. It's not that I'm some sort of sexual Superman; rather, it's because I've taken to heart what I read in that book and I really try to put my wife's pleasure and experience ahead of my own.

Distractions

Beyond the struggle with selfishness, there's also a general battle with distractions that often impedes the emotional intimacy that every marriage relationship needs. Look at it this way. When the average couple gets married, they don't have much money and they don't have much stuff. All they have is each other, and they tend to focus more on one another. But as they go forward and begin to get some financial traction and broader interests, their emotional intimacy often decreases. I read about a crazy example while in Iraq a few years ago. Someone had written to "Dear Abby" with the following issue:

> *My friend 'Suzy's' husband recently got a pet monkey named 'Jocko.' He and the monkey play games together. The problem is he has now begun ignoring Suzy in favor of the monkey. When Suzy wants to talk, her husband says, 'I'd rather spend time with Jocko.' That's only the beginning. She told me that she and her husband no longer share the same bed. He says, 'Jocko needs my company,' and he sleeps with the monkey on the couch. He also has a special chair for Jocko at the table, etc.*[5]

I don't know about you, but if I tried that at my house we'd have one dead monkey on our hands. My wife would take him out quicker than you could say "Harambe"!

You might say, "No man would be that dumb!" Well, that example might be over the top, but how about a more down to earth example. Have you heard of the new word "phubbing"? It's basically a combination of the words "phone" and "snubbing," and it's defined as "the act of snubbing someone in a social setting by looking at your phone instead of paying attention to the person." In fact, there's a whole website dedicated to this subject, www.stopphubbing.com. Men, we might not ever get distracted by a primate named "Jocko," but it's amazing how often many of us have allowed our electronic devices to make monkeys out of us all!

Passivity

Another hurdle that confronts every man is passivity. This takes place when a man grows passive toward actively investing in his marriage. And because most men tend to be goal-oriented, this is a significant danger. Consider that the average man actively pursued his wife before they were married. But once the wedding took place, the man mentally began to move on toward some other thing he wanted to achieve. "After all," so he assumes, "I've got her in the bag and now I don't need to keep pursuing her." But nothing could be further from the truth.

Take the story of my dad, for example. He and my mom were married for 24 years. But throughout those years, he focused almost exclusively on his work and his interests at the expense of his family. In fact, he did very little to cultivate relationships and invest in his family. My mom tried in many ways to make the relationship work, but she usually only got indifference or emotional apathy from my dad. After 24 years, she was at the end of her rope and said, "I'm done. I want a divorce." At that point, like most men who have been emotionally passive over the long haul, my dad suddenly woke up and said, "No, no! Wait, wait! I'll do anything!" But the damage was done, and their marriage fell apart. He died 18 months after the divorce. The doctors said that he died from a heart attack. I personally feel like he died from regrets. Regrets that he didn't invest in his family relationships when he had the chance. Regrets that his priorities over the course of 24 years of marriage did not facilitate relationship-building with his wife and children. Those are terrible regrets to live with, aren't they? That's why I actively warn men about passivity. It's something with which most men wrestle.

Love

The last word that sums up the commander's intent for marriage is the word "love." This word springs from the passage in the New Testament we referenced earlier:

Submit to one another out of reverence to Christ. Wives, submit yourselves to your own husbands as you do to the Lord. . . . Husbands, love your wives as Christ loved the church and gave himself up for her, that he might sanctify her . . . that she might be holy and without blemish. In the same say, husbands ought to love their wives as their own bodies. He who loves his wife loves himself. After all, no one ever hated their own body, but nourishes and cherishes it, just as Christ does the church. (Ephesians 5:21-22, 25-29)

In what is perhaps the most pointed Bible passage addressed specifically to husbands, this series of verses highlights the love that a husband owes his wife. And this is not just an abstract emotion or a set of romantic feelings. This is a love that is grounded in the example set by Jesus Christ himself.

Anytime we turn our attention to this passage in Ephesians, most men want to make a beeline toward verse 22, where it says that wives are to submit to their husbands. But in doing so, we often overlook the command in verse 21 sets the stage for the entire passage: "Submit to one another out of reverence to Christ." This is an important guideline, not least because it essentially says that submission in marriage is mutual—that is, the wife submits to her husband and the husband submits to his wife. But then as we go further into the passage, we see clearly that while submission is to be mutual, it is not to be identical. Wives are to submit to their husband's leadership; husbands are to submit themselves to their wives needs. And what does every wife need from her husband? Every wife needs Christ-centered, self-effacing, spiritually-enriching, love from her husband.

Love Your Wife Sacrificially

We first see in this passage that husbands should love their wives sacrificially: "Husbands, love your wives as Christ loved the church and gave himself up for her." Notice that it doesn't say, " . . . as Christ *loves* the church and *gives* himself up for her"—as if to focus on what Jesus is doing for the church presently. Rather, we see the past tense used. That is to say, the focus is on what Jesus did on the cross and the powerful scope of his sacrifice there.

We already know what motivated Jesus to leave Heaven's glory and come to the earth to die on the cross: "Let each of you look not only to his own interests, but also to the interests of others. Have this mind in you which was also in Christ Jesus" (Philippians 2:4-5). Why is this important in the context of marriage? It's because, as we have already discussed, selfishness is the number-one marriage killer. That's right. Every marital problem that any couple has ever experienced ultimately has selfishness at its root. And nothing exposes selfishness more than the close, intimate relationship of marriage. For example, after about six months of marriage, my wife said, "I never knew how selfish I was until I got married." And boy was she ever selfish! In fact, my wife was the second most selfish person I've ever known. But do you know who the most selfish person was? Me. So if selfishness is the number-one marriage killer, then what is the number-one marriage healer? A concern for your wife above and beyond your self-concern is the number-one marriage healer.

In referencing the death of Christ, the passage likewise highlights the "when" of a husband's love for his wife. We can illustrate the value of this concept by asking these questions: "When did Jesus Christ die for you? When you were at your very best? Or when you were at your very worst?" The answer, of course, is, "Jesus Christ died for me when I was at my very worst." We know this is true based on this text: "God demonstrates his love for us in that while we were yet sinners Christ died for us" (Romans 5:8).

Jesus died for you and for me when we were at our very worst. And that's exactly how we are to love our wives—when they are at their very worst. Oftentimes when preachers cover this passage from Ephesians, they will say, "You should love your wife enough that you would die for her." Have you ever heard that? Yes, we should. But if we're willing to die for our wives, why are we not so often willing to live for them? In fact, I think it's easier to die for your wife than it is to live for her. If you die for her, it's a one-time sacrifice and then you're gone. But if you live for her, it's something you do day after day after day. It's not easy, but it is the key to loving your wife sacrificially and the key to a true marriage that reflects the glory of God, peace, righteousness, and legacy.

Love Your Wife Spiritually

So what exactly is the purpose of a husband sacrificing himself for his wife? The purpose is that, just as Jesus "sanctified the church," the husband might "sanctify" his wife. That term "sanctify" means basically "to set apart as holy." This is not a frequent term in Paul's letters—it's primarily a priestly term used in connection with sacrifices. (Not surprisingly, in the New Testament it's found primarily in the book of Hebrews.) But Paul uses it to describe the influence of a person upon his or her spouse. For example, in 1 Corinthians 7:14 we see this statement: "An unbelieving husband is sanctified by his believing wife, and an unbelieving wife is sanctified by her believing husband." Of course, every analogy has its limits and this one does, too. But in a nutshell, Paul tells husbands that, through their example in word and deed, their wives ought to be a better, more radiant Christian.

Men, can that be said of you? Do you have that kind of influence and impact upon your wife? Or are you like the typical Christian husband who's basically along for the ride while his wife drives the spiritual car? Are you setting the spiritual pace in your home, or are you letting your wife assume that responsibility?

You may not currently be the spiritual pace setter in your home, but may I suggest that there are some simple, non-threatening ways that you could begin to change that. First, pray for your wife, and ask her how you can pray for her. Then make it a habit of praying for her each day—and then tell her regularly that you are praying for her. Second, make regular, consistent church attendance a priority for your family. Don't wait until you have nothing else taking place on Sunday (that is, no sports, trips to the lake, or other activities). Rather, determine in your heart that going to church will be a priority. And tell your family so. Let them know that you feel that this is a leadership responsibility given from God and that you are following what the Lord has led you to believe. Third—and perhaps the most powerful for your marriage—pray with your wife. Lead her in prayer. Hold hands, bow your heads, and ask God to bless your marriage and your home. You will be surprised how powerful this spiritual intimacy can be!

Love Your Wife Emotionally

When the words "nourish" and "cherish" appear in Ephesians 5:29, they speak of meeting needs in meaningful and compelling ways. In fact, the Greek word translated "cherish" appears only one other time in the New Testament, but it's occurrence is significant: "We were gentle among you, like a nursing mother taking care of her own children" (1 Thessalonians 2:7). In other words, a husband is to tenderly care for his wife with love and affection, meeting one of the greatest needs she has. This is not always easy for a husband to do, but few things will give greater rewards and contribute to the wellbeing of his marriage.

This is why we said that while submission in marriage is mutual it is not identical. The husband especially is instructed to meet his wife's needs with emotional nurturing and love. The challenge is that this is not always what the husband wants from his wife, so he's not necessarily inclined to give it. The old joke goes something like this: "Women want to be loved, to be listened to, to be desired, to be respected, to be needed, to be trusted, and sometimes, just to be held. And what do men want? Tickets to the Super Bowl." On a more serious note, Willard Harley in very important book *His Needs, Her Needs*, has highlighted the needs that most women desire: "affection, honesty, communication and openness, and family commitment."[6]

Yes, admittedly, loving our wives emotionally is a challenge. And I'm reminded of this on a regular basis as I observe couples interact. Some time ago, I was a chaplain at Fort Bragg, North Carolina with the Army's 82nd Airborne Division. One of my young Paratroopers was involved in a terrible motorcycle accident. He was comatose in a Greensboro hospital and his parents traveled from Montana to be at his bedside. When they arrived at the hospital, I escorted them to his room and they saw him there—unresponsive and hooked up to numerous machines. Now, his parents were plain "folk," just salt-of-the-earth people with an endearing air of rural simplicity—she was a schoolteacher and he was a small-engine mechanic. His mother stood next to her son and understandably broke down with uncontrollable sobbing. Meanwhile, the husband just stood at the foot of the bed about five feet away from his wife with his hands in his pockets. I'm sure he was engaging in his own coping mechanism, but I felt like saying to him, "Go over there and put your arm around your wife and comfort her you knucklehead!" Of course, it's easy to criticize someone else and see where he could have done a better job. But what about us? Are we living for our wives by nurturing and cherishing them?

Fortunately, every once in a while, a man does the right thing by recognizing his wife's need and then meeting that need in a loving and tender way. I read this short vignette in a book by Richard Selzer, *Mortal Lessons: Notes in the Art of Surgery*:

I stand by the bed where a young woman lies, her face post-operative and her mouth twisted in palsy—clownish. A tiny twig of the facial nerve, the one to the muscles of her mouth has been severed. She will be thus from now on. The surgeon followed with religious fervor the curves of her flesh—I promise you that. Nevertheless, in order to remove the cancer in her cheek, I had to cut the little nerve. Her young husband is also in the room; he stands on the opposite side of the bed. Together, they seem to dwell in the evening lamplight, isolated from me . . . private. Who are they? He and this young maiden, who gaze at and touch each other so generously and greedily. The young woman speaks, 'Will my mouth always be like this?' 'Yes,' I say, 'it will. It's because the nerve was cut.' She nods in silence. Then the young man smiles and says, 'I like it. It's kind of cute.' All at once I know who he is. I understand, and I lower my gaze. Unmindful, he bends to kiss her crooked mouth, and I, so close, can see how he twists his own lips to accommodate to hers—to show that their kiss still works. I say nothing; I hold my breath and let the wonder in.[7]

9

Fathers Lead the Way: Developing Influence With Your Kids

We've already said that God has appointed men as leaders in this world, and perhaps a man's greatest leadership calling is the opportunity to lead and influence his children. Indeed, as we mentioned in chapter one, a man's greatest impact on this world will likely be the legacy he leaves. A man's legacy will stretch far beyond his own lifetime, and when a more elite man determines that he will have a positive leadership impact upon his children, then his legacy may very well send a shockwave of peace and righteousness across time itself.

The most powerful means by which a man establishes his legacy is through leadership influence with his children. In fact, a father's primary role is that of influencer. Through various means, fathers influence their children in a powerful way. And, while your child will come under the influence of many things in his or her first 18 years of life, no other influence will have a more lasting impact than your influence. Of course, this cuts both ways. We've already seen that a father can influence his kids in a positive or negative way. And you as a father will be no different. The question is: how will you do it?

This chapter begins with an assumption—namely, that you as a dad want to have a positive influence on your children. And it also assumes that you want to lead the way and set the pace for this in your family. The following content offers some very practical examples for following through on that desire. Pay close attention. Your legacy depends on it.

A Vision for Influencing Your Child

Influence is a process; it doesn't happen overnight. You can only cultivate influence over time—months, years, and decades. Consistency is the key.

In order to understand influence, we must understand the relationship between influence and authority. Influence never forces itself; that is the role of authority. Yes, you can tell your child to mow the grass, take out the trash, or do their homework. But you cannot force them to do the most important things in life like loving God, loving other people, and walking in the truth. You can only *influence* them to do those things.

Several years ago, I read a very important book written by Ted Tripp entitled *Shepherding a Child's Heart.*[1] I learned several key lessons on raising children from reading the book, but the most significant take-away was about the relationship between parental authority and parental influence. And, as I read the book, I was challenged and encouraged to cultivate positive influence in the lives of my children.

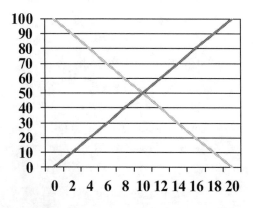
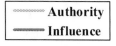

Shepherding a Child's Heart highlights the relationship between parental authority and influence. Specifically, parental authority declines as children get older, but positive parental influence with children (potentially) increases. If it appeared in terms of a graph, the vertical axis represents power or quantity of the item that is measured, and the horizontal axis represents the age of your child in terms of years. The solid line represents the amount of authority you have in your child's life at any given age. As you might suspect, the amount of authority you have in your child's life is going to decrease over the years. After all, when your child is, say, 4 years old, your relationship with that child is almost entirely a relationship of authority. But when your child is 17 years old, you won't have the same level of authority that you did when he or she was 4. And, by the way, the "authority" line is a solid line, because a decrease in authority as your child gets older is certain—there's nothing you can do about it, and it will happen no matter what.

On the other hand, the dashed line represents the amount of influence that you (potentially) will have with your child. I say "potentially" because there's no guarantee that you will ever cultivate influence with your child—and that's why it's shown in the form of a dashed line. It's not guaranteed.

Needless to say, the chart shows the dire need for dads to cultivate influence with their children. Because as a dad if you don't, then you have nothing left when your son or daughter is grown. No relationship. No desire on your child's part to consult you for wisdom. No hope that your legacy as a man will be carried on by your child.

The prospect of a father having no influence in the life of his 20-year-old son or daughter sounds pretty devastating to me. And that's one of the reasons why I'm such a big proponent of cultivating influence with my children. It's one of the reasons why influence is a huge part of my parenting vision.

How about yours?

How Do I Cultivate Influence?

The logical question at this point is, "How do I cultivate influence with my kids?" It's a great question that I wish more parents were asking. The answer is pretty simple. And the best way that I know how to express it is in terms of a mathematical equation.

I cannot tell you how much I disliked math as a kid. (Truth be told, I'm wild about it now, either.) But I've found over the years that sometimes the best way to express an idea like parental influence is through a mathematical equation. So here's my formula for cultivating influence with your children:

$$INFLUENCE = (Truth + Example^2) \text{ x Affection x Time}$$

So what does all of this really mean? Truth speaks of the words and lessons that you share with your child, especially as they come from God's Word, the Bible. Example speaks of the life that you live in front of your child. The reason why example is "squared" (that is, multiplied by itself) is because the life that you live and the example that you set for your child (good or bad) have twice the impact of the words that you share with them. Affection speaks of how you interact with your child, verbally and physically, in such a way as to demonstrate your unquestionable love for them. As the formula shows, this quality multiplies the power of your words and example. And finally, there is time. This speaks of the amount of time that you interact with your child. In this formula, the sum total of everything else is multiplied by the time that you actually spend with your children.

Sounds complex? Well, it's not really all that complicated. So let's unpack this formula in hopes that we can all cultivate deeper influence with our children.

TRUTH: Teaching Your Children the Ways of God

Every father has a primary responsibility to train and teach his children the Word of God and the ways of God. Yes, there are others who can partner with you in that endeavor, people like youth pastors, Bible teachers, and other godly families. But a father can never outsource his primary responsibility of teaching his children the truth about God. Or as I tell my kids, "Whatever you learn about God outside of our home is going to be gravy compared to the meat and potatoes you learn about God from me!"

The irony in my formula is that truth seems to have the least amount of force and power. After all, truth, by itself, multiplies nothing, and it's not multiplied by itself. But—and here's the irony—the most important part of influence is truth. The highest priority is on the truth. After all, if a father says, "I have no greater joy than to know that my children are walking in the truth" (3 John 4), then teaching that truth must take the primary place in the process of influence. The idea is not, "I have no greater joy than to take my son fishing" or "I have no greater joy than to give my daughter a hug." Yes, all of those things are enjoyable and satisfying to parents everywhere. But we must keep in mind that the other aspects of influence—example, affection, and time—are ultimately the setting in which a father communicates the truth with his children. In other words, building relationships with your children through fishing trips or hugs are *means to an end*, not ends unto themselves. On the other hand, without the other qualities of the formula, the truth that a dad shares with his child pretty much goes in one ear and out the other. But, if a dad has invested in his child's life through example, affection, and time, then his child will likely not only listen to the truth, but he or she will also seek out and crave their dad's instruction and advice about the truth. And isn't that what every dad should want—to have his child value and ask for his wisdom?

The idea of teaching truth is a deliberate process of transferring knowledge and instruction about God from one generation to the next. We often hear of the precarious nature of transferring wealth from one generation to the next—maybe your parents are getting nervous because they're now getting to the point of transferring wealth to you! But how much more important is it to transfer truth from one generation to the next? Think about this principle, for example, in terms of transferring spiritual truth (Psalm 78:1-6):

Oh my people, hear my teachings; listen to the words of my mouth. What we have heard and known—what our fathers have told us. We will not hide them from our children. We will tell the next generation about the praiseworthy deeds of the Lord, his power, and the wonders he has done. He commanded our forefathers to teach their children, so the next generation would know them, even the children yet to be born, and they in turn would tell their children. Then they would put their trust in God and keep his commands.

This is a strong mandate about sharing the truth with our children and the generation to come. But what does this mandate imply? Among other things, it implies that we as dads know for ourselves God's truth about character, integrity, and all that makes life worth living. Otherwise, how can we ever share it with our kids?

Additionally, there's a very important idea grounded in this concept of priority upon God's spiritual truth, and it has to do with the relationship between a spiritual desire for our children and a spiritual priority for our children. Do you know the difference? Fundamentally, every dad has desires for his children. In most cases, those desires revolve around things like academic success, social adjustment, athletic victory, spiritual health, and other sorts of things . . . all of which are good and commendable. But as a dad, you can only have one priority for your child. The question is, what is your priority for your child? In many cases, dads don't think in terms of priorities and desires, but all you have to do is look at where and when you most eagerly invests your time and treasure into your child and you'll see where your priority lies.

I'm certain that if you're reading this book you probably have numerous desires for your child. As mentioned above, you want your child to do well in school, in sports, in church, with friends, and with money. But the question is, "What is your priority?" The problem with many dads today is that they have a spiritual desire for their child, but they do not have a spiritual priority for their child. In other words, God is just one of many things going on in their child's life. But God doesn't want to be one of many things going on, he wants to be the main thing going on. But many dads are more interested in their children hitting a home run, winning a track meet, or shooting a big deer. Again, those are all wonderful milestones to enjoy together, but God never intended for them to be the priority.

I've found over the years that a simple little diagram I call "parenting above the dotted line" is a helpful reminder of the difference between desires and priority.

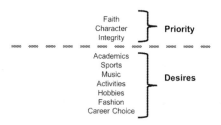

You basically take out a sheet of paper and draw a dotted line across the paper horizontally. They you write your priority for your child above the line and write your desires below the line. Then you determine in your heart to make the priority a no-fail part of your parenting strategy. Of course, you invest in your desires, too. But you also recognize that it's OK if your child doesn't measure up to every one of your desires. After all, at the end of the day your kids get a vote, too.

The best part of this little drawing is that it reminds us that our child's spiritual well-being is to be our priority, not just one of our desires. It aligns very well with Psalm 127:1, which says, "Unless the Lord builds the house, it's builders labor in vain."

Dad, can I speak to you frankly here? Why do you think so many dads don't have a spiritual priority for their children? I believe the number-one reason is that they don't have a spiritual priority for themselves. That's right. Oh, many have a spiritual desire for themselves—that is, they believe in God and want their children to have God in their lives, too. But if most dads were honest with themselves, they would admit that God is just one of many things going on in their lives, too. But God wants to be number-one in your life just as he wants to be number-one with your children. When you as a dad put God first in your life, you set conditions for a spiritual priority for your children, too.

EXAMPLE: Someone is Watching You!

Although truth is the first part of the formula that is listed—and it is indeed the most important part of the formula—perhaps the most penetrating part of cultivating influence with your children is the example that you set. Albert Schweitzer believed so strongly in the power of example that he wrote, "Example is not the main thing in influencing others; it's the only thing."[2] Well, as you might guess, I like to add a few other things into the equation besides just example. But Schweitzer's words remind us just how powerful an example really is. And there's no other aspect of the formula that can potentially wreck every other aspect more than a negative example, especially if dad is a hypocrite. But, on the other hand, a life well lived in front of your children will do more to cultivate influence than anything else.

Think about how important example really is. When it comes to expectations for our children, the fact is we cannot realistically expect our children to turn out any better than we are—whether we're speaking in terms of physical, emotional, or spiritual qualities. (Truth be told, they might not even turn out as good as you!) Taken another way, I'll say that your children will turn out just like you (or maybe worse!) unless there is some kind of external influence (for example, someone else they know outside of your home). And you just can't count on a positive external influence to enter your child's life these days, can you? It *might* happen, but don't bank on it. In fact, the influences that come into your child's life from outside of your home will likely be negative—and why would anyone want to gamble with their child's life by hoping that the external influences will carry the day?

So where do we begin when it comes to setting an example? I read a great little book on raising children a few years ago written by Michael and Debbie Pearl titled *No Greater Joy*. It's filled with all kinds of wisdom about being a parent (and I would recommend it to everyone who has the responsibility of raising children), but the greatest part of the book spoke of setting an example. The authors don't pull any punches when they write, "Decide what kind of person you want your child to become—and then become that person."[3] Isn't that great advice? Doesn't it make perfect sense? How simple, yet how elusive!

Isn't it amazing how closely our children are watching us? They pick up on the slightest things and then incorporate them into their own lives. They pick up our words, our habits, our idiosyncrasies, and even our personalities. Have you ever thought about one of your dad's quirks and said, "I'll never turn out like my dad!"—only to find out, years later, that you have the same quirk? And usually you're not even deliberately trying to emulate him. It just happens.

Hey, that brings up a great point. Probably more than any other aspect of influence, example has a potential for what I call a "delayed detonation." As I mentioned above, oftentimes a child will not make decisions about their own life—based upon mom and dad's example—until many years down the road. And that is why we should never give up doing the right thing in front of our kids, even if it seems like we're pouring water on a rock with no penetration whatsoever. Chances are, they *will* come around, even if it doesn't seem like they're paying much attention when they're young. Think about that famous verse from the Bible about raising kids: "Train up a child in the way that he should go, and when he is old he will not depart from it" (Proverbs 22:6).

Years ago, the song "The Cat's in the Cradle" was a popular song. It spoke about a man who doesn't have time for his young son because of a heavy workload and so forth. Then, after the little boy grows up to be a man, he, in turn, doesn't have any time for his dad. The last couple of lines from the song pretty much tell the whole story: "And as I hung up the phone it occurred to me, he's grown up just like me. My boy was just like me."[4]

Strive and endeavor to present a life well lived before your children. Start as early as possible. Otherwise, by the time your habits have been adopted by your children, it may just be too late to make a difference.

AFFECTION: Demonstrate Your Love

If we're going to cultivate influence with our children, we must show them affection—in word and in deed. And this isn't always easy, especially for men. Many of us just didn't get that kind of affection when we were kids. But that's no excuse. There's just too much at stake for us to cop out and say, "My dad never told me 'I love you'" or "My dad never hugged me."

Verbal affection is vital if you're going to cultivate influence with your children. And, regardless of how you were raised, you as a dad desperately need to learn how to say "I love you" to your children.

Have you ever noticed that some people just can't bring themselves to say that? My dad was like that. I could probably count on one hand the number of times that he actually said that to me in 25 years— and I might have 1 or 2 fingers left over! My dad, like a lot of dads, would sometimes say, "Love ya" or "Love you" (although even that was rare).

Hey, we don't say that to our kids; we say that to our dogs!

Probably even more important than verbal affection is physical affection. How often did you get hugs from your dad? Probably not often enough. It's a shame that not everyone in our generation has decided to "draw a line in the sand" and do something that our parents' generation often failed to do. I guarantee that you won't regret your decision to show your affection and love to your child through appropriate touch, hugs, and kisses.

And what about the relationship between affection and a child's emotional development and well-being? Did you know, for example, that young men desperately seek verbal affirmation from their dads? And when they don't get it, they often spend the rest of their lives seeking verbal affirmation from other men. And did you know that a lack of physical affection from a father often influences a daughter's decision to give herself away to other men sexually—oftentimes to men much older than themselves? Girls typically crave affection, and if they don't get it from their dads, then they'll go somewhere else to get it.

It's important that we take advantage of our opportunities to show verbal and physical affection while we can, because we never know when it will be too late. Chuck Swindoll, in his sermon entitled

"Essential Glue for Every Couple to Apply," tells a moving story that I quote at length here because of its power:

The salmon nearly leaped onto their hooks, which was a far cry from the day before when the four anglers couldn't even seem to catch an old boot. Disappointed but not discouraged, they had climbed aboard their small seaplane and skimmed over the Alaskan mountains to a pristine and secluded bay where the fish were sure to bite. They parked their aircraft and waded upstream where the water teemed with ready-to-catch salmon. Later that afternoon, they were surprised to find the seaplane high and dry. The tides fluctuated 23 feet in that particular bay, and the pontoons rested on a bed of gravel. Since they couldn't fly out until morning, they settled in for the night and enjoyed some of their catch for dinner.

In the morning, the seaplane was adrift, so they cranked the engine and began to take off. Too late, they discovered that one of the pontoons had been punctured and was filled with water. The extra weight threw the plane into a circular pattern. Within moments, the aircraft careened into the sea and capsized. Dr. Phil Littleford determined that everyone was alive, including his 12-year-old son, Mark. No safety equipment could be found on board—no life vest, no floats, no flares, no nothing. The plane sank into the icy morning sea. The frigid Alaskan waters chilled their breath. They all began to swim for shore, but the riptide countered every stroke. The two men alongside Phil and Mark were strong swimmers, and they both made shore. Their two companions last saw Phil and Mark as a disappearing dot on the horizon, swept arm-in-arm out to sea.

The Coast Guard reported that they probably lasted no more than an hour in the freezing water. Hypothermia would chill the body functions, and they would just go to sleep. Mark, with a smaller body mass, would fall asleep first . . . in his father's arms. Phil could have made the shoreline on his own, but that would have meant abandoning his son. Their bodies were never found.[5]

Can you imagine what that man said to his son as he embraced him before they sank? Can you imagine how tightly he hugged his boy?

At the end of that story, Swindoll asks, "Who wouldn't be willing to die for his son? But, if we are willing to die for our children, why are we not always willing to *live* for them?"

I'm sure we can all appreciate the power of the story and of Morley's question, but how many of us are really willing to live for our children through verbal and physical affection? You've got just a few precious years to build a meaningful relationship with your children. They grow up so quickly, don't they? So why not get with it and *tell* them and *show* them how much you love them? It may just seem like a small step, but it could be a giant leap toward cultivating powerful and meaningful influence with your children.

TIME: Give Presence to Your Kids

As dads, we probably struggle more with the issue of time than with any other aspect of influencing our kids. In fact, I am taking great care in writing this passage, because there's probably no other topic that can potentially send us all on guilt trips like the topic of time. After all, we have very demanding jobs, and probably none of us feels like we get enough time with our families. Sometimes we get extra time here and there, but, by and large, there just doesn't seem to be enough time to go around.

TIME: Do You Get The Point?

I'd like to think that every father understands how important time with his children is when it comes to influencing them. After all, if the entire formula for influence is multiplied by the time that we spend with our children, then our whole hope of cultivating that influence stands or falls on the amount of time that we spend with them.

Have you already made up your mind about your time priorities with your children? I hope so. But if not, let me share something that might get you thinking:

Where did the years go? I remember talking to my friend a number of years ago about our children. Mine were 5 and 7 then, just the ages when their daddy means everything to them. I wished that I could spend more time with my kids then, but I was too busy working. After all, I wanted to give them all of the things that I never had when I was growing up. I loved the idea of coming home and having them sit on my lap and telling me about their day, but, unfortunately, most days I got home so late that I was only able to kiss them good night after they had gone to sleep.

It's amazing how fast kids grow up. Before I knew it, they were 9 and 11. I missed seeing them in school plays. Everyone said that they were great, but the plays always seemed to go on when I was traveling for business or tied up in special conferences. The kids never complained, but I could see the disappointment in their eyes. I kept promising that I would have more time . . . next year. But the higher I climbed up the corporate ladder, the less time there seemed to be.

Suddenly, they were no longer 9 and 11; they were 14 and 16—teenagers. I didn't see my daughter the night she went out on her first date or my son's championship basketball game. Mom made excuses, and I managed to call on the phone and speak to them before they left the house. I could hear the disappointment in their voices, but I explained as best I could.

Don't ask where the years have gone. Those little kids are now 19 and 21. They're in college—I can't believe it. My job is less demanding now, and I finally have time for them, but they have their own interests and there isn't much time for me. To be honest, I'm a little hurt. Seems like yesterday they were 5 and 7. I'd give anything if I could live those years over—you can bet your life I would live them differently. But they are gone now, and so is my chance to be a real dad.[6]

If you're anything like me, you read that article and feel a little guilty. Like a lot of guys, I travel for work more often than I'd like. Of course, the man who wrote the article represents a radical form of family neglect. But even the thought of my children someday not having time for me—in large part, because I didn't have time for them—is enough to send a chill down my spine. So I'm pretty motivated to carve out as much time for them now as I possibly can.

What about you?

TIME: Some Practical Ways to Give Presence

OK, so you see where I'm going with this time thing. But how does a dad in this day of relentless hustle really carve out time to spend with his kids? Yes, there are just going to be some days when a dad—any dad—has to say "no" to his kids for the sake of his job. I totally understand this. Nevertheless, there are some practical ways that even the busiest of men can give their kids some meaningful presence.

One of the key principles I've tried is to minimize the amount of time that I spend away from my family while I'm off from work. When I'm off, I could be out playing golf or hunting or fishing with guys from work or other friends—all activities that I love doing. But how does that help me to build influence with my children? That doesn't mean that I don't head to the woods or get on the golf course with my buddies from time to time. After all, I need some of that for my own mental health and well-being. But ultimately I try to minimize those kinds of activities when they take me away from my family. When my children were small, I focused more on doing simple things together rather than doing things that I wanted to do on my own or with friends. Now that my kids are a bit older, we can do things together on the lake or in the woods. That's really the best of both worlds!

Tony Dungy, former coach of the Super Bowl Champion Indianapolis Colts, has said it in a similar way:

Every year since 1984, when our first daughter was born, I have tried to figure out, given the time demands on NFL coaches, how I could maximize my family time. When I went to work for the Kansas City Chiefs in 1989, the work hours increased even more. One of the things I decided to give up was golf. Although I enjoyed playing, I was never very good at it; and we had such limited time off in Kansas City that I couldn't justify not being home when I got the chance. I've never started playing again. Maybe, however, if one of our younger children takes up the game and needs a playing partner or a caddy—we'll just have to see.[7]

The key, I think, is to remember that the activities themselves are only a means to building relationships with my kids. If I put a higher priority on the activities themselves, then I might become annoyed that I have to set them aside while my kids are small. But when I see that the activities are only a means to an end—whether we're fishing or just going for a walk around the neighborhood—then I'll be content in knowing that we're together, regardless of what we're doing. For example, two of my boys and I were recently driving home from a dove hunt. We were talking about spending time together and how much fun they had on that hunt. I said, "Boys, I do enjoy hunting. But that's just the setting for the story. The story is us being together. As long as we have that story, I don't care about the setting."

I remember vividly what a man from my hometown shared with me a few years ago. He told me about a hunting trip that he and his teenage son experienced together. I asked, "Bob, did you grow up hunting?" He said, "Not too much. But when my son started showing a serious interest in getting out in the woods, I said to myself, 'I need to get into this, too, so that I can spend time with my son.'" I can remember being very impressed with that man's perspective, and I'm sure his son really appreciated it, too.

On that note, I had a professor in Chicago who shared some similar words of wisdom with me. He was a very busy man. In addition to teaching the writing books, he was also a part-time lumberjack. But he still found time to coach his teenage son's Little League baseball team. He said to me:

You know, a lot of people think that they've got to spend a ton of time with their children when their kids are really young, but then as the kids get older and kind of get on 'auto pilot' the parents don't have to spend as much time with them. But the opposite is true. You can get away with spending less time with them when they are very young, but as they get older you've got to spend more and more time with them.

I marveled at that man's wisdom, too, and I hoped that I could incorporate some of what he shared into my own life as a dad.

Another principle that I've found profitable is to make the most of little, mundane things that I can do with my children. This is especially helpful when your children are small. If I have to get gas for my truck, I'll take one or two of them with me—and usually I'll get them a little treat at the gas station, too. Or, if I have to go to town to buy something, no matter how small it is, I'll get one of them to ride along. If I'm traveling for work and there's a way that I can take one of my kids with me, then we make that happen, too. The bottom line is that I try never to go someplace alone when I could take at least one of my children with me. And, more often than not, they are very eager to go—especially when I offer to get them treats while we're out. Think back: you *remember* that kind of stuff as a kid, don't you?

Influence: Your Ticket to Happiness

After reading this chapter, I hope that you've gotten the idea that cultivating influence with your children will lead to happiness and peace of mind down the road. If nothing is more painful than being rejected by your children later in life, then there is nothing greater than moving from the job of parenting to the relationship of mentor, friend, and confidant as your children get older. Few things are harder on those getting up in years than the misery of living with regrets about how they raised their kids. Nobody's perfect—least of all me—but I you've begun to build a vision for influencing your kids while the time is ripe.

10

How to Get a GO with God: The Greatest Question a Man Will Ever Answer

"Roster number 180!"

The words echoed through the darkness of the Florida woods, and my heart started beating faster. I sounded off with a loud "Moving!" and ran into the darkness to where I heard the voice. I thought to myself, "Today could be the day. Today could be the day!" It was day 3 of our field training exercise in the Florida Phase of Ranger School, and I knew that if I could just get a "GO" that day, I'd have my Ranger Tab in the bag.

For a Ranger student, the most coveted words are, "Ranger, you're a 'GO' at this station." When you're in Ranger School, nothing else really matters, except to know that you're a "GO" and that you've made it.

Getting a Spiritual "GO"

Life is a lot like that, too. But now I'm not talking about Ranger School, I'm talking about your relationship with God. You could have everything in the world going for you, but if you miss that key relationship, what do you *really* have? Here's what Jesus said about it:

> *What should it profit a man if he should gain the whole world, and lose his soul?* (Matthew 16:26)

Now, if we were using the language of Ranger School, maybe we could ask this question: "How do I get a "GO" with God?"

And isn't that the biggest question of them all—isn't that the most important "GO" that anyone could get? Let's talk about it.

FAITH is the Key

In the Vietnam War, a young Ranger officer named Bobby Welch fought the Viet Cong and nearly died in the process. As a long-range platoon leader, he earned a Bronze Star with "V" device, a Purple Heart, and the Combat Infantryman's Badge. But more than that, he experienced a spiritual transformation as a part of his combat experience that changed his life forever.[1]

Bobby Welch left the Army and became a minister. He understood that he had gotten a "GO" with God, and he wanted to help others to get their "GO," too. He came up with a simple way to explain to others how they could experience the same blessing that he had, and he used the simple word F-A-I-T-H as an illustration (it's perfect for Rangers, really, since we're so in love with acronyms). Forty years later, Bobby's simple explanation of how to get a "GO" with God has helped tens of thousands of people to make a life-changing decision.[2]

I'd like to share it with you here, because there truly is nothing greater, nothing higher than a relationship with God.

"F" is For Forgiveness

Getting a "GO" with God begins with forgiveness—namely, God's forgiveness for our sins. After all, as the Bible tells us, we're all sinners and because of that sin all we're separated from God: "All have sinned and have fallen short of God's glory" (Romans 3:23). Fortunately, God sent Jesus to the earth that we might have forgiveness through him:

> *In Jesus, we have redemption through his blood—namely, the forgiveness of our sins—according to the riches of God's grace.* (Ephesians 1:7)

But what's up with this blood stuff? Well, God began to show that forgiveness comes through the shedding of blood when he prescribed animal sacrifices for his people in the Old Testament:

> *Without the shedding of blood, there is no forgiveness.* (Hebrews 9:22)

Then, God presented the ultimate means of forgiveness when Jesus died on the cross. In fact, that's why he was called "Jesus" in the first place: "The angel said, 'You shall call him "Jesus," because he will save his people from their sins" (Matthew 1:21).

So it all starts with "F"—it all starts with forgiveness.

"A" is For Available

The second letter in the word "F-A-I-T-H" stands for "available"— that is, forgiveness is available through Jesus Christ. And the really good news is that it's available to *everyone*, as the most famous verse in the Bible tells us:

For God so loved the world that he gave his one and only Son, that whosoever believes in him should not perish but have everlasting life. (John 3:16)

Yes, God's forgiveness is available to everyone, everywhere. There's no one who cannot receive God's forgiveness if they want it.

But, God's forgiveness is not automatic.

You know, in America we tend to believe that everybody goes to Heaven—well, except for Hitler and maybe Stalin. But it's not true. And even Jesus said so in the famous Sermon on the Mount:

Jesus said, "Not everyone who says to me, 'Lord, Lord,' will enter the kingdom of Heaven. Many will say to me on that day, 'Lord, Lord' . . . and I will tell them plainly, 'Depart from me, you evildoers! I never knew you.'" (Matthew 7:21-23)

I'm so glad that God's forgiveness is available to everyone, aren't you? But, as we've heard from Jesus' own mouth, it's not automatic. Or to put it another way, there's something that has to happen before we can get our "GO" with God.

But what?

"I" is For Impossible

Next we see that "I" is for "impossible." But what is impossible? Well, we see in the Bible that it's impossible for sin to enter into Heaven:

Nothing impure will ever enter Heaven, nor will anyone who does what is shameful or deceitful, but only those whose names are written in the Lamb's Book of Life. (Revelation 21:27)

Of course, this presents a problem for you and for me, right? As we've already mentioned, we're all sinners. So that means we can't get into Heaven.

Or can we?

"T" is For Turn

OK, we're in a real mess now. First, we see that God's forgiveness is not automatic, and now we see that it's impossible for sin to enter into Heaven. Is there any hope for us?

Yes, and it begins with the word "turn."

Let's suppose we're driving out in Columbus, Georgia and you come to a one-way street that goes to the left (and not to the right). Now let's suppose that for whatever reason, you mistakenly take a right turn onto that one-way street (maybe you're texting or whatever). How long will it take for you to know that you're going the wrong way on a one-way street? Probably just a few seconds. So then what do you do?

You turn around, right?

That's the picture the Bible presents of someone who receives God's forgiveness—it's the picture of a person who figures out that they're going the wrong way and decides to turn around so that they're going the right way.

Another word in the Bible for turn around is "repent," but the picture is still the same:

Repent and turn to God, so that your sins may be taken away and so that times of refreshing may come from the Lord. (Acts 3:19)

God commands all people everywhere to repent. For he has set a day when he will judge the world with justice by the man he has appointed. (Acts 17:30-31)

Everyone should repent and turn to God and prove their repentance by their deeds. (Acts 26:20)

So here's the key: we receive God's forgiveness and find a way to enter Heaven by turning—by repenting. But turning is not just about turning away from going in the wrong direction (namely, doing things *our* way rather than God's way). Turning is also about turning toward someone perfect and loving and holy and good. Turning is about turning toward Jesus. But how exactly do we make the decision to turn? It's a *free gift* that we must receive.

First, God's gift of forgiveness if FREE. Years ago, I conducted a funeral for an elderly woman named Helen in my civilian church. The funeral lasted 2 hours, and I only spoke for 5 minutes. Mostly, the funeral was a parade of people who had known her, each sharing wonderful things about her. I already had my sermon all planned out, but after hearing all of these comments, I "called an audible" on myself. Instead, I got up and said, "You know, Helen was indeed a wonderful person. But I get the sense that some people here are thinking, 'She was such a good person. Surely she's in Heaven today.'" Then I said, "*If* Helen is in Heaven today—and I truly believe that she is—then she's not there because of all of the good deeds that she did. She's there because of what Jesus did for her on the cross—and because she accepted that gift of forgiveness."

You know, that's exactly what the Bible says, by the way. What verse did I read at that funeral service? This is what I read:

At one time we were foolish, disobedient, and enslaved by all sorts of passions and pleasures. But when the kindness and love of God our Savior appeared, he saved us, not because of righteous things we had done, but because of his mercy. (Titus 3:3-5)

But not only is God's forgiveness FREE, it's also a GIFT that we need to receive. After all, if I had a beautifully-wrapped gift with your name on it, you would have to physically receive it from me in order to have it and enjoy it, right? The same goes for God's gift of forgiveness and salvation:

> *To everyone who received Jesus—to those who believed in his name—to them he gave the right to be called children of God.* (John 1:12)

So what really happens when you "turn"—when you repent? You turn away from your sin and you turn toward Jesus Christ to receive his gift of forgiveness and salvation.

But what exactly does that really mean for your life and mine?

"H" is for Heaven

After you decide to turn to Jesus and receive his gift of forgiveness and salvation, you experience Heaven in a very real way. But don't get the idea that Heaven is just someplace in the great "hereafter." Yes, Heaven is a place that God has prepared for us for a future time. But Heaven—if you've received God's free gift of forgiveness and salvation—is also here and now.

First, let's look at the present. Do you remember the key verse we mentioned earlier, John 10:10? It's where Jesus said, "I have come, that they might have life." Well, was he talking about some time in the distant future, or was he talking about life here and now? Of course, he was talking about life here and now.

I personally turned to Jesus Christ over 25 years ago, and I can say without any doubt in my mind that life is better when Jesus is at the center of your life—your marriage, your relationship with family, your job, everything. And just to know Jesus Christ on this earth, regardless of what happens in the distant future, is awesome. I like how one man said it: "I'd be a Christian even if there were no Heaven or hell."

Hey, life is hard enough even when we do have God in our lives. Why would anyone want to live life without him?

But, as we've already said, Heaven is also a place that God has prepared for us at a future time. Jesus himself said so:

Do not let your hearts be troubled. Trust in God; trust also in me. In my Father's house are many rooms; if it were not so, I would have told you. I am going there to prepare a place for you. And if I go and prepare a place for you, I will come back and take you to be where I am. (John 14:1-3)

What first got me thinking seriously about my standing with God was a question that someone asked me over 25 years ago: "If you died tonight, do you know with absolutely certainty that you would be in Heaven?" At the time, I only had answers like "I hope so" or "I don't know." As I learned in the days after hearing that question, the Bible says that we can *know for certain* if we're going to Heaven.

These things I have written that you who believe in the name of the Son of God might know that you have eternal life. (1 John 5:13)

Now we know that if this earthly tent in which we dwell is destroyed, we have a building from God, an eternal house in Heaven not built by human hands. (2 Corinthians 5:1)

I've spent a lot of time in Iraq and Afghanistan with the Rangers (not to mention I jump out of planes with them, too), and I would be a fool to do that on a regular basis without a solid certainty of God's forgiveness and salvation. There have been many times when I have reminded myself of the simple confidence found in that second verse: "We know we have . . . an eternal house in Heaven."

F-A-I-T-H: Are You a GO or a NO-GO?

So there you have it. F-A-I-T-H. It makes the difference between being a "GO" or "NO-GO."

Where are you in all of this? Are you a "GO"? Are you a "NO-GO"? Maybe you're certain; maybe you're not.

I would guess that there are probably three kinds of men reading this book:

First would be those men who have never trusted Jesus Christ—those who have never turned from their sin and received God's gift of forgiveness and salvation. There are many in this category, and maybe you're one of them. Maybe you've thought about it before, or maybe this is the first time you've ever heard what we've talked about in this chapter. Either way, you're only one prayer away from receiving that wonderful gift. Here's how Bobby Welch put it:

> *A pastor helped me to pray what's affectionately called "the sinner's prayer": "Dear Jesus, I believe that you died on the cross for my sins and that you rose from the grave. I now ask you to forgive me of my sins, come into my life, and save my soul." It was maybe the first time I ever really prayed. Most of the things I was praying about I did not understand very well. But the Lord understood that I wanted my life to change.[3]*

Second, there are many men who grew up in a Christian home but who, for whatever reason, have gotten away from that. This is not uncommon—and it's not new, either. I knew several guys just like that when I was enlisted in the Marines 25 years ago. But the good news is that *it's never too late to do the right thing*, and it's never too late to say to God once again that you want your life to belong to him.

In the 1800s, Queen Victoria reigned in England for almost 65 years. Early in her life as the Queen, a young man from India came to visit her in London. He was a Punjab prince who brought a magnificent diamond to the Queen as a gift. The stone, commonly known as the Kohinoor diamond (which means "mountain of light"), was over 186 carats in weight! As the largest diamond in the world, it was made a part of the Queen's Crown Jewels.

Years later, that same man—now much older—visited the Queen in London. Much to the surprise of the British leadership, he said, "I want to see the Kohinoor diamond." They thought, "Why does he want to see it? Does he want it back?!" So they went to the Tower of London to see the jewel. As the man, the Queen, and others stood there, he said, "Put it in my hands"—and everyone thought, "Uh oh, here it comes." After he was handed the stone, he turned to the Queen and spoke these words:

> *When I was a child, I gave you this diamond. At the time, I was very young and didn't fully understand its worth or why I was giving it to you. But now, with years of experience and wisdom, I understand better just how valuable this stone really is. And so . . . I want to give it to you one more time.*[4]

You know, that may describe how you feel right now. At one time, you gave your heart and life to Jesus Christ, but either you didn't really understand then what you were doing or else you've gotten away from that kind of sincere devotion and now you want to get back to it. Either way, there's no time like the present to say to God, "I want to give you my life one more time."

And third, let's not forget that some of you are currently living the Christian life—you're "walking the walk"—which is no small accomplishment. I give thanks for your commitment and your steadfast faith, and I pray that you would continue to honor God with your life. And as you read the words of this chapter and recall how your own life with Jesus Christ started—wherever and whenever that was—give thanks to God for all that he has done in your life!

Draw Near to God!

Regardless of who you are, never forget these encouraging words found in the Bible:

Draw near to God and he will draw near to you. (James 4:8)

I pray that the content of this book has allowed you to do just that—to draw near to God. After all, God's wisdom and power are at the heart of a more elite life. And, as you draw near to the Almighty Creator of the universe in a personal and loving way, I pray that your life would be changed for the better in ways that you can't even imagine.

Endnotes

Introduction

[1] Stanley McChrystal, *My Share of the Task: A Memoir* (London: Portfolio, 2013), 72.

[2] Patrick Morley, *The Man in the Mirror* (Grand Rapids: Zondervan, 1997).

[3] Steve Farrar, *Point Man* (Colorado Springs: Multnomah, 2003).

[4] Alex and Stephen Kendrick, *The Resolution for Men* (Nashville: Broadman & Holman, 2011).

[5] Chuck Holton, *A More Elite Soldier* (Colorado Springs: Multnomah, 2003); Jeff Struecker, *The Road to Unafraid* (Nashville: Thomas Nelson, 2009); John MacDougall, *Jesus Was an Airborne Ranger* (Colorado Springs: Multnomah, 2014).

Chapter One

[1] John D. Lock, *To Fight With Intrepidity: The Complete History of the U.S. Army Rangers 1622 to Present* (New York: Simon and Schuster, 1998), 9-11.

[2] Stephen Arterburn, *Every Young Man, God's Man* (Colorado Springs: Waterbrook, 2010), 282.

[3] Stephen Covey, *Seven Habits of Highly Effective People* (New York: Free Press, 1989), 5.

[4] James Loehr and Tony Schwartz, *The Power of Full Engagement* (New York: Free Press, 2003), 133.

[5] Michael Hyatt and Daniel Harkavy, *Living Forward: A Proven Plan to Stop Drifting and Get the Life You Want* (Grand Rapids: Baker, 2016), 57-67.

[6] Suzy Welch, *10-10-10: A Life Transforming Idea* (New York: Scribner, 2009).

[7] James MacDonald, "Decision Time," Walk in the Word, accessed November 2, 2016, https://store. jamesmacdonald.com/p-1018-decision-time.aspx.

[8] "Cranky Man Shoots Lawn Mower for Not Starting," NBC News, accessed October 14, 2016, http://www.nbcnews.com/id/25854715/ns/us_news-weird_news/t/cranky-man-shoots-lawn-mower-not-starting.

Chapter Two

[1] Army Demotes 'Swinging General' After Investigation Into Affairs, Lifestyle," USA Today, accessed December 16, 2016, https://www.usademotes-swinging-general-david-haight/9549.

[2] Army General Apologizes to Victims of Misconduct Before Being Sentenced," New York Times, accessed December 16, 2016, https://www.nytimes.com/2014/03/20/us/general-apologizes-to-sexual-misconduct-victims.html?mcubz=1.

[3] "Army Recommends no further Punishment for Petraeus," The Washington Post, accessed December 7, 2016, https://www.washingtonpost.com/world/national-security/army-recommends-no-punishment-for-petraeus-after-receiving-doj-materials/2015/12/07/2a31d43e-9867-11e5-94f0-9eeaff906ef3_story.html?utm_term=.48771e4c1009.

[4] Hyatt and Harkavy, *Living Forward*, 32.

[5] Alexander Solzhenitsyn, *The Gulag Archipeligo 1918-1956* (London: Harvill Press, 2003), 176.

[6] Maria Popova, "The Best Insights from Stephen Covey's '7 Habits of Highly Effective People,'" The Atlantic, accessed January 3, 2017, https://www.theatlantic.com/entertainment/ archive/2012/07/the-best-insights-from-stephen-coveys-7-habits-of-highly-effective-people/259990.

[7] Stephen Mansfield, *Paul Harvey's America: The Life, Art, and Faith of a Man Who Transformed Radio and Inspired a Nation* (Chicago: Tyndale, 2011), 102.

[8] "Tiger Woods' Apology," CNN, accessed February 19, 2016, http://www.cnn.com/ 2010/US/02/19/tiger.woods.transcript/index. html.

[9] Dean C. Ludwig and Clinton O. Longenecker, "The Bathsheba Syndrome: The Ethical Syndrome of Successful Leaders," *Journal of Business Ethics* (April 1993): 265-273.

[10] Lewis Sorley, "The Way of the Soldier: Remembering General Creighton Abrams," Foreign Policy Research Institute, accessed December 12, 2016, https://www.fpri.org/article/2013/05/the-way-of-the-soldier-remembering-general-creighton-abrams.

[11] Geoffrey Chaucer, *The Canterbury Tales* (New York: Penguin, 2003), 16.

Chapter Three

[1] Charles Swindoll, *Hand Me Another Brick: Building Character in Yourself and Others* (New York: Bantam Books, 1983); Frank Page, *The Nehemiah Factor: 16 Characteristics of a Missional Leader* (Birmingham: New Hope Publishers, 2008).

[2] Jason Kirby, "Why Business People Won't Stop Using That Gretsky Quote," Macleans, accessed September 24, 2016, http://www.macleans.ca/economy/business/why-business-people-wont-stop-using-that-gretzky-quote.

[3] Travis Smith, "Mrs. Disney: 'He Did See It; That's Why It's Here,'" LinkedIn, accessed January 21, 2017, https://www.linkedin.com/pulse/channel-reminder-mrs-disney-he-did-see-thats-why-its-here-smith.

[4] John Maxwell, "How Do I Change My Mindset from That of a Producer to That of a Leader?" The John Maxwell, accessed January 6, 2017, http://www.johnmaxwell.com/blog/how-do-i-change-my-mindset-from-that-of-a-producer-to-that-of-a-leader.

[5] Andy Stanley, *Visioneering: Your Guide for Discovering and Maintaining Personal Vision* (Colorado Springs: Multnomah, 2005), 123.

[6] Michael Catt, "And Pray and Seek His Face," Sherwood Baptist Church, accessed April 29, 2017, http://sherwoodbaptist.net /media/sermons/and-pray-and-seek-his-face/205.

[7] Adrian Rogers, "The Blood Covenant," Love Worth Finding, accessed March 12, 2016, https://www.youtube.com/watch?v=JssBBA1vngk.

[8] Joey Johnston, "The Wit of John McKay," *Tampa Bay Times*, June 17, 2010, http://www.tbo.com/sports/bucs/the-wit-of-john-mckay-34909.

[9] Brian Jones, "There Is No Substitute for Hustle," Senior Pastor Central, accessed August 28, 2016, http://seniorpastorcentral. com/3021/theres-no-substitute-hustle.

[10] Michael Catt, "The Leader and His Integrity," Sherwood Bapist Church, accessed February 21, 2016, http://sherwoodbaptist. net/media/sermons/the-leader-and-his-integrity/163.

[11] Ibid.

Chapter Four

[1] Brian M. Thomsen, ed., *The Man in the Arena: Selected Writings of Theodore Roosevelt* (New York: Forge Books, 2004), 12.

[2] Theodore Roosevelt, *Fear God and Take Your Own Part* (New York: George Doran Company, 1916), 24.

³ William Blacker, "Oliver's Advice," in *The Dublin Book of Irish Verse 1728-1909* (Dublin: Hodges, 1909), 30.

⁴ Adrian Rogers, "How to Turn Your Problems Into Possibilities," Love Worth Finding, 1978, author's collection.

⁵ Cited by Ravi Zacharias, *The Grand Weaver* (Grand Rapids: Zondervan, 2010), 24.

⁶ Elbert Hubbard, *A Message to Garcia* (East Aurora: Roycroft, 1899).

⁷ Stephen Ambrose, *Nothing Like it In the Whole World* (New York: Simon & Schuster, 2001).

⁸ Ravi Zacharias, "A Willful Walk," Just Thinking, accessed September 25, 2016, http://rzim.org/just-thinking/a-willful-walk.

⁹ Roy P. Basser, ed., *The Collected Works of Abraham Lincoln*, Vol. 6 (New Brunswick: Rutgers University Press, 1953), 158.

¹⁰ Douglas MacArthur, "Radio Address, September 2, 1945," Battleship Missouri Memorial, accessed March 13, 2017, https://ussmissouri.org/learn-the-history/surrender/general-macarthurs-radio-address.

¹¹ Patrick Morley, "What To Do When the Novelty Wears Off," Patrick Morley, accessed December 23, 2016, October 17, 2014, http://patrickmorley.com/blog/2014/10/12/what-to-to-when-the-novelty-wears-off.

¹² Colin Welland, *Chariots of Fire*, DVD, directed by Hugh Hudson (1981; Hollywood: Warner Brothers, 1997).

[13] Robert Klemko, "If Winning or Losing is Going to Define You, You're On a Rough Road," The MMQB with Peter King, accessed February 1, 2016 (https://ww.si.com/mmbq/2016/01/31/nfl-mmbq-bud-grant/Minnesota-vikings-super-bowl-losses-vince-lombardi-dislike); John Walters, "Bud Grant: The Meanest Nicest Man In NFL History," *Newsweek*, May 20, 2015, http://www.newsweek.com/2015/06/05/bud-grant-meanest-nicest-man-nfl-history-333853.html.

[14] Patrick Morley, *The Man in the Mirror*, 74.

[15] William Ernest Henley, "Invictus," Poetry Foundation, accessed December 22, 2016, https://www.poetry foundation.org/poems /51642/invictus.

[16] Stephen Tompkins, *John Wesley: A Biography* (Grand Rapids: Eerdmans, 2003), 190-198; John Wesley, *The Journal of John Wesley*, ed. Percy Livingstone Parker (Chicago: Moody Press, 1951).

Chapter Five

[1] G. K. Chesterton, *The Collected Works of G. K. Chesterton*, Vol. 1, ed. Lawrence J. Clipper (San Francisco: Ignatius, 1989), 588.

[2] Duncan Campbell, "Vanuatu Tops Wellbeing and Environment Index," The Guardian, accessed July 12, 2016, https://www.theguardian.com/world/2006/jul/12/healthandwellbeing. lifeandhealth.

[3] John Bogle, *Enough: True Measures of Money, Business, and Life* (New York: John Wiley & Sons, 2008), 184.

[4] Dave Ramsey, "The Truth About Budgeting," Dave Ramsey, accessed December 19, 2016, available from: https://www. daveramsey.com/blog/the-truth-about-budgeting.

[5] Dave Ramsey, "Seven Signs Your Budget Needs a Fresh Start," Dave Ramsey, accessed December 19, 2016, https://www. daveramsey. com/blog/7-signs-your-budget-needs-fresh-start.

[6] Dave Ramsey, "Dave Ramsey's Seven Baby Steps," Dave Ramsey, accessed December 19 2016, https:// www.daveramsey.com/baby-steps.

[7] Dave Ramsey, *Total Money Makeover* (Nashville: Thomas Nelson, 2009).

[8] Ron Blue, *Never Enough?* (Nashville: Broadman & Holman, 2017), 132.

[9] James MacDonald, "Breaking the Addiction to Debt," Walk in the Word, accessed June 29, 2016, https://www.jamesmacdonald. com/ teaching/devotionals/2009-06-29.

[10] "Debt-Induced Stress Continues for Many Americans," Newsmax, accessed June 1, 2016, available from: https://www.newsmax.com/ Finance/InvestingAnalysis/US-AP-Poll-Stressing/2010 /06/01/ id/360713.

[11] Morley, *The Man in the Mirror*, 24.

[12] Deborah Jacobs, "Winning the Lottery Isn't Always a Happy Ending," *Forbes*, December 18, 2013, https://www.forbes.com/sites/

deborahljacobs/2012/11/28/winning-the-lottery-isnt-always-a-happy-ending/#45d431c733ab.

[13] Ron Dicker, "10 Star Athletes Who Excelled at Losing Millions," AOL.com, accessed September 19, 2016, https://www.aol.com/2011/09/19/10-star-athletes-who-excelled-at-losing-millions.

[14] Bogle, *Enough*, 68.

[15] Paul Davidson, "Americans Are Saving Less As Income Lags Spending," *USA Today*, August 9, 2017, https://www.usatoday.com/story/money/2017/08/09/americans-saving-less-income-lags-spending/549177001; Charisse Jones, "Millions of Americans Have Little to No Money Saved," *USA Today*, March 31, 2015, https://www.usatoday.com/story/money/personalfinance/2015/03/31/millions-of-americans-have-no-money-saved/70680904.

[16] Kimberly Palmer, *Generation Earn* (New York: Emeryville, Ten Speed Press, 2010), 124.

[17] Dave Ramsey, "The Miracle of Giving," Financial Peace, accessed June 9, 2012, https://www. youtube.com/watch? v=yt_xO_j1e-E.

Chapter Six

[1] "Ranger Athlete Warrior: Further, Faster, Fight Harder," 75th Ranger Regiment, Fort Benning, Georgia, accessed December 20, 2016, http://www.benning.army.mil/tenant/75thranger/content/ PDF/ Intro%20Brief.pdf.

[2] Carl Gustav Boberg, *How Great Thou Art* (Monsteras Tidingen, 1885).

[3] Don Harris, *Lord Most High* (Integrity Music, 1996).

[4] Michael S. Hamilton, "The Dissatisfaction of Francis Schaeffer," *Christianity Today*, March 3, 1997, http://www.christianitytoday. com/ct/1997/march3/7t322b.html.

[5] Jessica Durando, "10 Inspiring Quotes by Mother Theresa," *USA Today*, August 26, 2014, https://www.usatoday.com/story/ news/ nation-now/2014/08/26/mother-teresa-quotes/14364401.

[6] Tim Henderson, "Number of People Living Solo Can Pose Challenges," Pew Trust, accessed September 11, 2016, http://www. pewtrusts.org/en/research-and-analysis/blogs/stateline /2014/09/11/ growing-number-of-people-living-solo-can-pose-challenges.

[7] Matthew E. Brashears, Miller McPherson, and Lynn Smith-Lovin, "Social Isolation in America: Changes in Core Discussion Networks over Two Decades," *American Sociological Review* 71, accessed December 15, 2016, http://happierhuman.wpengine. netdna-cdn.com/ wp-content/uploads/2014/06/ P13.-Social-Isolation-in-America- Changes-in-Core-Discussion-Networks-over-Two-Decades.pdf.

[8] "Albert Schweitzer's Leadership for Life," AlbertSchweitzer. com, accessed January 21, 2017, http://aschweitzer.com/about a.html.

<u>Chapter Seven</u>

[1] Stu Weber, *Tender Warrior* (Colorado Springs: Multnomah, 2006), 141.

[2] Isabel Sawhill, "20 Years Later, It Turns Out That Dan Quayle Was Right About Murphy Brown," *Washington Post*, May 25,

2012, https://www.washingtonpost.com/opinions/20-years-later-it-turns-out-dan-quayle-was-right-about-murphy-brown-and-unmarried-moms/2012/05/25/gJQAsNCJqU_story.html?utm_term=.2a34c0754ad6.

[3] Aaron Parsley, "Jennifer Aniston: Women Don't Need Men to Be Good Moms," *People*, August 8, 2010, http://people.com/celebrity/jennifer-aniston-women-dont-need-men-to-be-good-moms.

[4] "Jennifer Aniston Slammed For Suggesting Dads Are Optional In Families," Fox News, accessed August 10, 2016, http://www.foxnews.com/entertainment/2010/08/10/jennifer-aniston-slammed-suggesting-women-dont-need-man-start-family.html.

[5] "Father Facts," All Pro Dad, accessed February 2, 2017, http://www.allprodad.com/father-facts.

[6] Bill Madden, *Steinbrenner: The Last Lion of Baseball* (San Francisco: Harper, 2010).

[7] Ibid, 25.

[8] Ibid.

[9] Ibid.

[10] Ibid, 22.

[11] Adrian Rogers, "Dads Who Shoot Straight," Love Worth Finding, 1996, author's collection.

[12] Eric Ludy, *God's Gift to Women* (Colorado Springs: Multnomah, 2003), 24.

[13] James MacDonald, "Blessing," Walk in the Word, accessed March 11, 2017, https:// jamesmacdonald.com/teaching/ devotionals/2013-03-11.

[14] John Trent and Gary Smalley, *The Blessing* (Nashville: Thomas Nelson, 2011).

[15] Michael Kimmel, *Manhood in America: A Cultural History* (Oxford: Oxford University Press, 2011), 153.

[16] Robert Mendick, "Raoul Moat: 'I've No Dad, No One Cares About Me,'" *The Telegraph*, July 11, 2010, http://www.telegraph. co.uk/ news/uknews/crime/7883742/Raoul-Moat-Ive-no-dad-no-one-cares-about-me.html.

[17] Tami Rudder, "Fatherhood: The Changing Family Photo," Gallup News, accessed April 9, 2016, http://news.gallup.com/poll /5773/ fatherhood-changing-family-photo.aspx; "Fathers In America," Gallup News, accessed April 9, 2016, https://www. fact.on.ca/rel_ supp/gallup.htm.

Chapter Eight

[1] Abby Elin, "After Full Lives Together, More Older Couples are Divorcing," *New York Times*, October 30, 2015, https://www. nytimes.com/2015/10/31/your-money/after-full-lives-together-more-older-couples-are-divorcing.html?mcubz=1.

[2] Tommy Nelson, "Love Song," Denton Bible Church, 1993, http://www.dbcmedia.org/ sermons/love-song-a-study-in-the-song-of-solomon.

[3] Jill Savage, "Seven Ways to Develop Emotional Intimacy in Your Marriage," Crosstalk, accessed December 20, 2016, http://www.crosswalk.com/family/marriage/seven-ways-to-develop-emotional-intimacy-in-your-marriage-11642928.html.

[4] Cliff Penner and Joyce Penner, *How to Get Your Sex Life Off to a Great Start* (Nashville: Thomas Nelson, 1994).

[5] "Monkey Stirring Up Trouble," *Houston Chronicle*, December 17, 2006, http://www.chron.com/life/article/DEAR-ABBY-Monkey-stirring-up-trouble-1904684.php.

[6] Willard Harley, *His Needs, Her Needs* (New York: Revell, 2002).

[7] Richard Selzer, *Mortal Lessons: Notes in the Art of Surgery* (San Diego: Harcourt Brace, 1996), 45.

Chapter Nine

[1] Tedd Tripp, *Shepherding a Child's Heart* (Wapwallopen: Shepherd Press, 1995).

[2] Albert Schweitzer, *The Thoughts of Our Times* (Mount Vernon: Peter Pauper Press, 1975).

[3] Michael Pearl and Debbie Pearl, *No Greater Joy, Volume 1* (Pleasantville: No Greater Joy Ministries, 1997).

[4] Harry Chapin, *Cat's In the Cradle*, (Elektra, 1973).

[5] Chuck Swindoll, "Essential Glue for Every Couple to Apply," Insight for Living, accessed April 5, 2007, http://store. insight.org/p-746-essential-glue-for-every-couple-to-apply.aspx.

[6] Ibid.

[7] Tony Dungy, "An Open Letter to Dads from Tony Dungy," Lifeway Articles, accessed June 7, 2016, http://www.lifeway.com/Article/Tony-Dungys-tip-for-all-fathers.

<u>Chapter Ten</u>

[1] Bobby Welch, *You, the Warrior Leader* (Nashville: Broadman & Holman, 2004).

[2] Bobby Welch, *Evangelism Through the Sunday School: A Journey of Faith* (Nashville: Lifeway, 1997).

[3] Welch, *You, the Warrior Leader*, 211.

[4] Adrian Rogers, "How to Discover Your Spiritual Gift," Love Worth Finding, accessed August 24, 2006, https://www.lwf. org/products/2203CD.

Please send any comments or question about this book to
chaplainkramer@yahoo.com. Also, go to www.philkramer.
org for additional teaching from Phil Kramer.

Printed in the United States
By Bookmasters